Christian Feminism

Christian Feminism

COMPLETING THE SUBTOTAL WOMAN

Mary Bader Papa

Fides/Claretian

Printed in the United States of America

ISBN 0-8190-0644-0

Cover design: Glenn Heinlein

Cover art: Will Bradley

LC 81-5368

First printing, July 1981

Fides/Claretian books are a series of books, published by the Claretian Fathers and Brothers, which examine the issue of Christian social justice in the United States. The books are written for grassroots Christians seeking social justice. They are based on the premise that it is not possible for everyone to do everything, but it is a Christian duty for everyone to do something.

For more information about Fides/Claretian, write to the address below.

221 West Madison Street • Chicago. Illinois 60606

TO JOEL,
MY HUSBAND

Contents

Acknowledgments

Many people helped me write this book. I am especially grateful to the anonymous women who have shared their stories with me. Thanks are due also to Evon Bachaus, Mary Kennedy Lamb, Catherine Mamer, the Minnesota Council for the Economic Status of Women, and the South Carolina Commission on Women for providing information. I am also grateful for the information provided by two priests, and I regret that I cannot name them for fear that their ecclesiastical careers might suffer as a consequence. And finally, I want to thank my family—my mother, Madeline O'Rourke Bader; my husband, Joel C. Papa; our children, Joel, Donald, Elizabeth, and Maria. Their love, support, and insights are invaluable.

Acknowledgment is also made for permission to quote from the following books:

From Machismo to Mutuality, by Rosemary Radford Ruether and Eugene Bianchi, published by Paulist Press, copyright 1976.

Women: New Dimensions, by Elisabeth Schussler Fiorenza, published by Paulist Press, copyright 1975.

Woman: Survivor in the Church, by Joan Ohanneson. Copyright 1980 by Joan Ohanneson. Published by Winston Press, Inc., 430 Oak Grove, Minneapolis Mn. All rights reserved.

Kiss Sleeping Beauty Good-bye, by Madonna Kolbenschlag, published by Doubleday, copyright 1979.

Foreword

At a time when many in the church are confused about issues raised by the women's movement, there is need for a clear analysis of sexism. Confronting "the lie of women's inferiority" is impossible without such an exposition. This book provides ample material not only for understanding the situation causing sexism today, but also for directing readers toward solutions.

As an auditor at the Second Vatican Council, I observed how the bishops were affected by movements which had been growing in the church for decades—ecumenism, the people as the church, the liturgical movement, religious liberty, and so on. But acceptance of the insights of the women's movement was barely discernible. True, the Council Fathers included the statement, "Every type of discrimination . . . based on sex . . . is to be overcome and eradicated as contrary to God's intent." But that text was almost the only indication that sexism is admittedly sinful.

I recall the clear and simple statement of a laywoman during an official meeting at the Council; she spoke quite fearlessly to the framers of the document on *The Church in the Modern World:* "You may omit all the pedestals and incense 'honoring' women. All women really want is to be treated in the church as the full human persons they are." Progress toward that reality is falteringly slow. But the encouraging sign is that many Christian feminists, affirming the profound values of their faith, are today willing to work to achieve full justice for women.

The first step toward any liberation is to recognize existing inequality. That is why Mary Bader Papa has done well to deal with the problem of sexism. If and when equality for women is realized in practice in the church, more profound changes will take place than any yet achieved in other areas. For the subordinate situation of women known as sexism exists as the primary root of every other domination.

Sociologists tell us that only when "countervailing trends" or opposition currents are widely enough communicated and understood, deeply enough grounded, and finally, accepted by the dominant opposing group, will social change take place.

Any dominance of some persons over others is an evil which has become more and more obvious today. As we read Scriptures now, old texts sparkle with sharp new relevance. "The rulers of the Gentiles lord it over their people. *But it shall not be so with you. . . .*"

Those who realize the importance of taking a first step toward creating a countervailing trend need tools of consciousness-raising to assist in the task. One reaches for a simple text, a "primer," to carry the persuasive message in a practical way, lay out the boundaries, confront the sticky issues, and propose strategies for advancing. This study by Mary Bader Papa provides just such a needed instrument. Judicious, compassionate, spicy, the text articulates women's uneasiness and anger, winning assent to work to overcome the evil of sexism.

The coverage of how the church can deal with injustice both inside and outside is one of the gems of this book. With a reporter's skill, Mary Bader Papa has not only listed with accuracy all the problems of injustice, but has provided energizing motivation along with reasons for hope.

When feminist writers like the author, seeing the need for profound social change, are able to articulate it, not in bizarre images, but in words in which women recognize themselves, assent is won and the first wave of change is under way. After this stage, movement can progress more rapidly. It seems to me that many women and a growing number of men in the Catholic Church are just now being caught up in building the countervailing trend. The cause of feminism needs speakers and writers like Mary Bader Papa who can name the inequities of sexism and point the way toward overcoming them. She writes with clarity and wit. Her pungent quips make the reading of this book highly entertaining. It is important to note that economic injustice, the core of much of the evil of inequality, is well documented throughout.

We all need this book. Bishops and clerics, made uneasy by the implications of the women's movement, should read it; it will assure them that they have urgent work to do, but that they have a blueprint for getting on with it. Educators, businesspeople, and politicians need it. The book can serve admirably, not only as a primer for beginners in correcting sexism, or a measuring stick for those in progress, but also as a beckoning vision for those who would achieve the goal indicated by the author in the final paragraph: "a balanced relationship of equality of women with men."

MARY LUKE TOBIN, S.L.

1

Justice for Women, Too?

Funny, but Justice was a woman.

When the old Greek and Roman gods were running the universe, Themis, goddess of justice, sat next to Zeus, the top god, and she held the scales of justice that kept an assortment of other gods and people in line.

Nowadays Justice is usually an old statue hanging around a courthouse somewhere. We recognize her instantly, because she is the one with the blindfold. It's supposed to mean that justice is blind, treating us all equally.

But a middle-aged woman walking out of a courtroom in which she has just been divorced might be forgiven for pushing the statue of Justice off its marble pedestal. To her, Justice is a blind fool. The blindfold is what keeps Lady Justice from recognizing *in*justice—injustice directed against other women.

Women have not thought so much in terms of injustice when talking of their own lives. They have thought in terms of fate. They have thought in terms of children, of love, of husbands, of singleness, of marriage, of heartbreak, and of living-happily-ever-after. They say things to one another about how this isn't fair or that isn't fair. They complain it isn't fair that they do more work and earn less money; that they cook the meals and do the clean-up, too; that their status depends entirely on some men's status—whose wives they are, whose secretaries they are, whose proteges they are. But injustice? That's a word they save for the *really* important problems such as racial prejudice, anti-Semitism, and anti-Catholic bigotry.

Women are quick to identify with the underdog—with children, with the poor, with the elderly. It's just generally assumed that women are more sensitive, kinder, gentler, and more suited to such concerns than men are. But is it so? Or is it that women have a natural tendency to identify with the powerlessness in others—rather than facing the powerlessness in themselves?

For some women, the civil-rights movement in the 1960s was a new awakening about the injustice on which their own lives were based. They thought they were joining a historic struggle for justice—and they were. But they also came to realize that their male compatriots in this cause, the very males who were struggling to assure black people their rightful places in our society, continued to regard their women companions as people worthy of an inferior place—servicing males with typewriters, coffee, or sex. In the midst of a struggle for justice for others, these women realized they had yet to struggle for justice for themselves.

Women and Slaves

The women of the 1960s who discovered their own need for liberation through civil rights work with American blacks were echoes of their sisters more than a century earlier. Those earlier advocates of women's rights, the women whose speeches and organizing eventually succeeded in winning the vote for American women, began as opponents of slavery. They soon realized their own powerlessness along with the powerlessness of slaves.

When the leading abolitionists met in Philadelphia in 1833, a few women were permitted to *attend* the meeting, but they were not permitted to *join* the American Anti-Slavery Society that resulted from the gathering of high-minded male reformers. (On reconsideration, maybe this is why the Lady Justice donned a blindfold: She couldn't stand to watch such stuff anymore.)

So the women formed their own antislavery organization, and when they held the first national convention in 1837, they suffered another affront. A leading male abolitionist offered to be the presiding officer. Assuring this gallant man that they could in fact run their own meeting, the women declined.

Early abolitionist women such as Angelina Grimke touched off an outcry by giving public speeches and petitioning government authorities on behalf of the antislavery movement. Women were not supposed to speak in public. It was scandalous. It was unladylike. It was un-Christian. As the Council of Congregationalist Ministers of Massachusetts put it:

> The appropriate duties and influence of women are clearly stated in the New Testament. Those duties, and that influence are unobtrusive and private, but the sources of mighty power. When the mild, *dependent,* softening influence upon the sternness of man's opinions is fully exercised, society feels the effect of it in a thousand forms. *The power of woman is her dependence,* flowing from the consciousness of that *weakness* which God has given her for her *protection* . . .
>
> But when she assumes the place and tone of man as a public reformer . . . she yields the power which God has given her *for her protection,* and her character becomes unnatural. If the vine, whose strength and beauty is to lean on the trellis-work, and half conceal its cluster, thinks to assume the *independence* and the overshadowing nature of the elm, it will not only cease to

> bear fruit, but fall in shame and dishonor into the dust. [Emphasis added]

Vines leaning on the trellis-work and half-concealing their clusters? Did Lady Justice have ear plugs as well as a blindfold?

Nevertheless the women continued to advocate women's rights along with abolition of slavery. Male abolitionists begged Angelina and her sister Sarah to drop the women's issue for fear that it would harm the antislavery cause—a fact which modern women ought to secure tightly in their minds, for they hear similar pleas today to lay aside "women's issues" until issues of higher priority are settled. Until we end the war. Until the economy improves. Until the election is over. Until.

But Angelina Grimke declined to set women's rights aside for the antislavery cause, and she wisely explained why not:

> We cannot push Abolitionism forward with all our might until we take up the stumbling block out of the road. . . . Why, my dear brothers, can you not see the deep-laid scheme of the clergy against us as lecturers? . . . If we surrender the right to speak in public this year, we must surrender the right to petition next year, and the right to write the year after, and so on. What then can woman do for the slave, when she herself is under the feet of man and shamed into silence?

But in seeing the injustice of women's lives along with the injustice of slavery, no one was clearer or more eloquent than a freed slave and abolitionist leader named Sojourner Truth. In 1851, she moved a partly hostile audience to tears at a women's rights convention in Akron, Ohio when she rose to answer a clergyman who said women were weak and ought not be given the vote:

> The man over there says women need to be helped into carriages and lifted over ditches, and to have the best place everywhere. Nobody ever helps me into carriages or over puddles, or gives me the best place—and ain't I a woman?

> Look at my arm! I have ploughed and planted and gathered into barns, and no man could head me—and ain't I a woman? I could work as much and eat as much as a man—when I could get it—and bear the lash as well! And ain't I a woman? I have born 13 children, and seen most of 'em sold into slavery, and when I cried out with my mother's grief, none but Jesus heard me—and ain't I a woman?

The evils of racism and sexism, leading as they do to the subjugation of some human beings to others on the basis of race or sex, were issues that belonged together. Those who struggled for rights for blacks and those who struggled for rights for women did not always see the compatability of their causes as clearly as Sojurner Truth did. But the search for justice was the same. The evils of racism and sexism are branches of the same root injustice in the human race. It is an injustice that says some people are inferior to other people.

The god who presides over this system did not create all men equal, even though the Constitution of the United States says so. That god created white men equal. He—and we can be certain *that* god was a "he"—did not create white women or people of any other color equal to white men.

And so people who want to work for equal justice for all

people cannot decide, for instance, that equality for women is an issue that ought not to be taken seriously because they decide it is of interest to "white, upper-middle-class women" whose problems in no way can be compared to the indignities suffered by blacks at the hands of the Ku Klux Klan. If they decide that discrimination against women is a peripheral issue, they do not really understand how tolerance of sexism injures the human family just as tolerance of racism does. Nor do they really understand how both evils have gone hand in hand in history, making humanity much less than it could have been.

Catholic bishop Joseph A. Francis, of Newark, N.J., who is black, has called his church to face the fact of its own institutional racism. "It is well and alive and very few institutions in our country have done less to combat racism, given its mission to witness to Christ's presence among us," he has said, pointing out that individual church leaders have publicly endorsed the marches of Martin Luther King and the strikes of Cesar Chavez, but they have not dealt with the racism built into their diocese, religious orders, universities, and other church organizations. "I fight against racism, not because I am one of its victims, but because we are all its victims."

Bishop Francis could well have said the same about sexism.

Just What's So Unjust About It?

"Look, I'm really sincere about this," the man says, leaning forward and trying not to betray his irritation. "Just what's so *unjust* about women's lives?" He pauses and invites your eyes to follow his eyes around the room, past the living room as handsomely furnished as any in *House Beautiful,* past his *wife's* dishwasher, through the window where his *wife's* car can be seen pulling into the driveway, returning his wife from an exhausting afternoon of racquetball. You are reminded by his facial expression that *he* is exhausted from a hard week of work and airline travel, complicated by another frustrating tie-up at O'Hare Airport that caused him to miss his connections, and so on: "I'd like to be playing racquetball myself!"

As he tells it, his wife has all the fun, and he has all the work. It may be that, as are many men in such an economic arrangement, he is a prisoner of the materialism that really runs their lives. Work, work, work to keep ahead of the pack, to buy the bigger house, the better car, the ski trips, the club memberships. His wife's role in this partnership is to do the shopping and provide the testimony that at least *one* of them is enjoying the products of his labor.

Another possible version of this scene is that this man's domestic life is another feather in his cap to show off along with his last promotion. *His* house, *his* wife. *He* pays for both of them. And when he acts chagrined that she is playing racquetball while he, poor soul, is racing from airport to airport, he is really indulging in bragging of sorts—letting it be known that he is the magnanimous person who finances such luxuries. The woman, in fact, is nothing without him. She exists to coordinate the scenery against which he plays his life—although the meaning of his life is somewhere else, usually in his job. Meaning in *her* life is a subject she tries not to think about. She settles for a meaningful activity, and so far what she has found is racquetball.

There are many excellent racquetball players (and tennis players and bridge players, too) in the metropolitan areas of America. Most of them play for recreation, of course.

But an uncomfortable number of them play for self-esteem. Most of the latter are privileged economically, but they have one important thing in common with the majority of poor people in this country: They are women.

Of the 25 million Americans who are officially poor, 10 million are women, 10 million are their children, and 5 million are men.

There is one underlying reason why women are poor. They are poor because they are trained from childhood to be dependent on the goodwill and generosity of men. And they have been trained since childhood to solicit that goodwill and generosity with beauty and charm, attributes they have sometimes developed at the expense of their other human attributes. They are trained to expect to be supported by a husband and steered into low-paying jobs, so that even when they are not supported by men they earn only about 60 percent of what men earn.

Trained to be dependent this way, a woman's life is activated or immobilized by whatever man she is hooked up to at a given moment. Whether she lives in House Beautiful or a roach-infested flat may really be beyond her control. All women share an element of chance in their lives. A joke that women savor these days as black humor asks, "Why don't women gamble as much as men do?" Because, the answer goes, women's total instinct for gambling is satisfied by marriage.

Women end up poor and undervalued in the labor market often as a result of having spent years at home raising families, for homemaking is a career that society values with its words but not with its laws and other tangible evidence of regard:

  • Property laws often disregard entirely the value of a

homemaker's contribution to family prosperity and well-being. In 1981, Georgia law still stipulated that the husband is "head of the family and the wife is subject to him."

● Under South Carolina law, a married man who owns only personal property (bonds, stocks, cash) in 1981 could still make a valid will leaving his wife nothing. Although a wife could do the same, a homemaker would ordinarily be more disadvantaged in such a situation than her husband. Furthermore, where there is no will, the wife may forfeit her "dower rights" (her lifetime interest in part of her husband's real estate) if she is guilty of marital "misconduct." There is no similar provision to punish a man for "misconduct."

● Until the law was changed in 1979, a husband in Louisiana could sell or mortgage the family home without consent or knowledge of his wife.

● In 1979, several middle-aged homemakers were hired as clerical workers at a Minnesota high school. They were paid the minimum wage, and the general attitude was that since the women were "just housewives" they ought to be grateful for a chance to earn some money. And the women *were* satisfied with the arrangement—until they found out that *boys* from the student body had been hired at *higher* wages to sweep floors after school.

● For their devotion to their families, women often end up poorer in old age than anyone. In 1979, the average income for women aged 65 and older was $3,700; for men it was $6,410.

The evidence of injustice in women's lives goes on and on. But the root of all women's woes is this: Their lives are based on lies—lies that stem from the original lie that women are inferior to men.

The original lie led of necessity to more lies to cover and

justify the original one. Elaborate theologies have been constructed to prove that the operative system of lies (the one which has been the status quo for so long) does not really say that women are inferior. ("Why, on the contrary," one Baptist minister said on television, "we believe women are superior." And that is why, he reasoned, his congregation opposed the Equal Rights Amendment.)

But the system that is sexism is a system constructed on a lie, nevertheless. And like the original malignant cell that multiplied viciously, it is a system that has become a cancer on the human race. It is not a woman's problem alone.

But People Are Starving in Africa!

One of the major changes taking place in our lifetimes is the movement for the equality of women and men—usually referred to as the women's movement, even though many men support it. There has been much misunderstanding about the women's movement, however. To its detractors it appears to be a selfish movement, a sort of group narcissism for women who care only about themselves. Others, somewhat more sympathetic, grant that the movement has some legitimate complaints but cannot see justification for trying to correct centuries of injustice in one decade.

How, they ask women, can you justify working for rights for yourself when people are starving to death in Africa? Or Brazil. Or South Bronx. Or when Palestinians are deprived of even the right to a homeland? Or when abortion results in all rights being denied to fetuses? Or when the world may self-destruct at any moment thanks to the wonder of nuclear energy? Their list—like the list of women's grievances—goes on and on. And the question behind each question on their list is the same: How can privileged American women even begin to compare their grievances to the pressing injustices that others suffer? In fact, how dare they?

If women have energy to devote to seeking social justice in the world, shouldn't they devote that energy to the really "serious" injustices that exist—the life-and-death issues, especially those on which the clock is running out? After a nuclear holocaust, what good is it going to do a woman to have an American Express card in her own name?

This sort of reasoning has worked very effectively on women for a long time. They were asked to set aside their own grievances so as not to hurt the antislavery cause. They have been asked throughout history to put the needs of husband, children, country, church—in short, anyone and anything—before their own. In doing so, they have served neither themselves nor others. Sexism still afflicts the human race.

In addition, some of those who suffer from "more serious injustices" have their agony compounded by sexism. In Africa where people really are starving to death, women's inferior position limits their access to the food that is available. A *Wall Street Journal* report from Zaire tells of a public health study there that found 34 percent of all children die of protein deficiency before they reach age five. In addition to poverty, sexist social custom is involved in this starvation. In Zaire, it is customary for men to eat first, then women and children. This is true even though women do all the domestic and agricultural work, and nurse babies.

Sexism is also explanation for an unspeakable cruelty inflicted upon little girls throughout much of Africa today—genital mutilation that includes cutting off the clitoris and other operations that result in permanent health damage, hemorrhage, infections such as tetanus, problems during childbirth, frigidity, painful intercourse, menstrual complications, and other disabilities. Fran P. Hosken, coordinator of Women's International Network, Lexington, Massachusetts has been trying to call attention to this abomination at the United Nations among other places. Hosken's investigations conclude that 30 million women and girls have been so mutilated. "The most dangerous operation, infibulation or pharaonic circumcision," she has written, "is practiced in Sudan, Somalia, and along the Red Sea Coast, as well as in Mali in West Africa. It means that after the exterior genital organs of the child are removed, the vagina is closed by scarification or sewing. The legs of the child are tied together for several weeks until the wound is healed, closing the vagina except for a small opening for elimination, created by a splinter of wood. *Thus, virginity, which is considered important by Moslem men, can be proved before the brideprice is paid.*" [Emphasis added] Among the many agencies that have ignored the World Health Organization's calls for a halt to such practices, is the U.S. Agency for International Development, which Hosken charges shuts its eyes to the fact that even AID equipment, paid for by U.S. taxpayers, is being used to perform this genital mutilation.

Stopping these atrocities is as much a part of the agenda for women as stopping the legal inequities in U.S. property laws. Sexism permeates the whole human family. Some of its manifestations are more odious than others, but they all are rooted in the same evil.

Yet some people trivialize the concerns advanced by the women's movement. They refuse to see the broad injustice that is manifested by specific instances of discrimination. If they don't minimize the seriousness of sexism with teasing remarks, they may imply that there are far greater problems that confront society.

Accusing women of selfishness seems to be a very effective way of immobilizing them—especially Christian women, trained to believe they should work for *others*. It is also a way of disparaging the efforts of Christian feminists, those women and men whose beliefs about equality derive from the teachings of Jesus Christ. Christian feminists do not see their work as selfish; rather, they see it definitely as work for *others,* those oppressed by sexism.

But Christians have explicit directions as to what sort of work they should be doing for others. It is spelled out rather neatly in the gospels. (In the past, the actual *implementation* of these teachings has been done disproportionately by female Christians while the *recognition* for their efforts has largely fallen to male Christians. But Christian feminists won't settle for that sort of arrangement anymore.)

Jesus—who ought to have more to say about what sort of behavior is necessary for Christians than anyone else—spelled it all out. This is what he expected of those who would follow him:

"For I was hungry and you gave me food, I was thirsty and you gave me drink. I was a stranger and you welcomed me, naked and you clothed me. I was ill and you comforted me, in prison and you came to visit me." But when, Jesus said the "just" people would someday ask, did they do all these things? And they would be told that as long as they did these things for one of the "least" people they did it for him. (Matthew 25: 35-40)

These directives, known as the works of mercy, clearly direct us to love our neighbor, to serve others. They even tell us how. There is no mistaking it. But in case we missed the point the first time, Jesus goes on to mention what he plans to say to the people who are not "just" when they stand before him for judgment:

"Out of my sight, you condemned, into that everlasting fire prepared for the devil and his angels! I was hungry and you gave me no food, I was thirsty and you gave me no drink. I was away from home and you gave me no welcome, naked and you gave me no clothing. I was ill and in prison and you did not come to comfort me." And again, they will want to know when they failed to do these things. "I assure you, as often as you neglected to do it to one of these least ones, you neglected to do it to me." (Matthew 25: 41-46)

There seems to be a clear mandate for action here—the kind of merciful justice Jesus himself practiced. Even a casual reading makes it clear that Jesus did not think it was enough to delegate such activity to the Women's Relief Society or the Christian Mother's Club. He wanted everyone involved.

A feminist will have to admit, on the other hand, that this explicit list doesn't mention anything about "I was for the ERA, and you worked for ratification" or "I wanted the Social Security laws reformed, and you lobbied your senator." It is fair to say that working for women's rights is not—at first glance—an obvious priority among the corporal works of mercy in Christianity.

And yet in Jesus' teaching mercy implies justice, as well. Mercy and justice are linked. Consider the Sermon on the Mount:

> Blessed are the poor in spirit, for theirs is the kingdom of heaven.

Blessed are the meek, for they shall inherit the earth.

Blessed are they who mourn, for they shall be comforted.

Blessed are they who hunger and thirst for justice, for they shall be satisfied.

Blessed are the merciful, for they shall obtain mercy.

Blessed are the clean of heart, for they shall see God.

Blessed are the peacemakers, for they shall be called children of God.

Blessed are they who suffer persecution for justice's sake, for theirs is the kingdom of heaven.

Blessed are you when men reproach you, and persecute you and, speaking falsely, say all manner of evil against you for my sake. Rejoice and exult, because your reward is great in heaven; for so did they persecute the prophets who were before you.

Justice is mentioned twice in this famous passage. No other virtue is mentioned twice. Blessed are both those who hunger for justice and those who are persecuted for the sake of justice. The final point is also an encouragement for those who seek justice, for their road is unlikely to be an easy one. Blessed are those who are reproached and persecuted and slandered for living up to these teachings of Jesus. Remember, he says encouragingly, they persecuted the prophets who came before you.

Therefore Christians who see the inferior status of women as an issue of justice believe that their struggle for equality is a prophetic struggle in line with the letter and the spirit of Jesus' teachings. In addition to literally feeding the hungry, giving drink to the thirsty, and so on, Christians compelled by justice go further. Their concern, as did Jesus' concern, goes beyond temporarily satisfying immediate needs. It also addresses the causes of those needs: the causes of their hunger, thirst, nakedness, homelessness, illness, and imprisonment.

Feminists, whether they are Christian feminists or not, usually look at the causes of women's problems, including the deprivations of hunger, illness, imprisonment, and more, and they see that these inequities can be traced to a system built on sexism. What they see is a society in which:

● The majority of people in poverty are women and their children.

● The overwhelming majority of those who are victims of family violence are women and their children.

● Among those most desperate for decent housing they can afford are women and their children.

The status of women and the children dependent upon them results from their basic powerlessness. And this powerlessness is the outcome of our social order which encourages girls to train for a life of dependency, which encourages women to turn the direction of their lives over to men, or to a series of men. It discourages women from being independent, from taking responsibility for determining their own directions in life. It saps the strength of self-determination that most little girls once had within them. And it punishes women when they try to recover that strength. And so, even with some advances made in recent years by the women's movement, women—and their dependent children—remain the most powerless people in society.

So is it selfish for feminists to work for women's rights—and ultimately for the equality of all people? Or is the selfishness among those who oppose equality? After all, those who oppose equality are usually those who stand to benefit in some way by keeping things the way they are. Feminists are only seeking justice. Where in Scripture is the seeking of justice called selfish?

In both the Jewish and the Christian heritages, there is a strong call to mercy grounded unequivocally in justice. It is easy for feminists to feel both vindicated and inspired by these words of Isaiah instructing people about fasting:

> Is this the manner of fasting I wish, of keeping a day of penance:
> That a man bow his head like a reed, and lie in sackcloth and ashes?
> Do you call this a fast, a day acceptable to the Lord? This rather, is the fasting that I wish:
> *releasing those bound unjustly,*
> *untying the thongs of the yoke;*
> *Setting free the oppressed, breaking every yoke;* Sharing your bread with the hungry, sheltering the oppressed and the homeless;
> Clothing the naked when you see them, and *not turning your back on your own.*
> Then your light shall break forth like the dawn, and your wound shall quickly be healed. . . ."
>
> (Isaiah 58: 5-8) [emphasis added]

Setting free the oppressed. Breaking every yoke. And not turning your back on your own. A feminist agenda.

In traditional religious practice, however, women tend to be confined to a narrow path of merciful work. In Mother's Day sermons and in pious religious literature, the true Christian woman is celebrated as a humble, gentle doer of good deeds for others. She cares for children and the elderly. She takes meals to the sick. She collects blankets for refugees. She raises money for the church through bake sales and bazaars—and she bites her tongue before ex-

17

Justice for Women, Too

pressing resentment that *men* will decide how to spend the
money she has made. This good woman who has given so
much to others, faithfully and selflessly, for so long, is now
offered reproachfully to feminists as a model.

This process of reproaching feminists—especially Christian feminists—reached a peak after Mother Teresa of Cal-
cutta received the 1979 Nobel Peace Prize for her heroic
works of mercy in the world's most oppressive centers of
poverty. To some people, Mother Teresa epitomized the
ideal of the selfless servant nun—the sort, they observed,
that there used to be more of before nuns became interested in modernizing themselves and so many of the nuns
in America began insisting on the power to control their
own lives, of all things! Churchmen wasted no time sug-
gesting that these uppity American nuns and all women
look to Mother Teresa for a model of what a woman ought
to be: humble almost to the point of unbelievability, selfless
in service to others, obedient to the male hierarchy. And
she didn't give a lot of speeches.

This last point about Mother Teresa proved especially
appealing to some people, in light of another nun named
Theresa.

In October of 1979, Sister Theresa Kane, then president
of the Leadership Conference of Women Religious, as a
representative of U.S. nuns was called upon to officially
greet Pope John Paul II during his visit to the United States.
She decided to use the occasion to forthrightly address the
Pope in public about the need to improve the status of
women within the Catholic Church. Sister Theresa's historic speech called forth a storm of criticism, despite the
brief and respectful manner in which she presented it.

Comparisons between Sister Theresa and Mother Ter-

18

esa, both prominent nuns—one dressed in a humble sari and veil, the other in a business suit—were inevitable. And most of the comparisons did a disservice to *both* women. Critics who assumed that by speaking up courageously for justice Sister Theresa was a stranger to mercy, or that in doing her heroic works of mercy Mother Teresa was somehow blind to injustice in the world trivialized the work of both women.

Many decent men and women who generously contribute to charity and volunteer their spare time to help others found it very hard to understand what Sister Theresa was saying to the Pope. In their eyes she was a nun who ought to be visibly helping the poor or teaching children or nursing the sick. Instead, they saw her as a privileged woman mouthing the "feminist party line" and concerned with the "selfish" interests of women. These critics did not comprehend the commitment to justice that had prompted Sister Theresa to speak that day. They could not comprehend the breadth of the injustice that she linked to sexism, and they could not comprehend the mercy she was showing to other women by using her position to speak the truth.

On the other hand, Mother Teresa was not universally appreciated by social activists, including some of those who have seen first hand the grossly unfair systems that perpetuate the poverty in which Mother Teresa works. Things are so bad that other people are moved to anger and then to politics in their attempts to change conditions that produce such horrors. But not Mother Teresa. She goes right on picking the hopelessly poor people off the streets, and the system keeps right on producing more victims. She is, in the eyes of some people, just another woman who bandages the wounds of capitalism, helping to stifle the natural urge among its victims to rebel against the system. But can they see nothing of justice in her global witness to the enormous scope of human misery? And is there nothing of justice in her efforts to heal the injustice of individual lives? It is unlikely that Mother Teresa will ever lead a political revolution against injustice, but isn't there something revolutionary about the scope of her love that is making a difference in places that more sophisticated, more educated people have written off as beyond hope?

Both Sister Theresa and Mother Teresa have much to teach us about mercy and justice—if only we would really listen to them instead of trying to manipulate their public images to conform to our personal ideas of what a woman's place should be.

Who Is More Blessed—The Meek Or Those Who Seek Justice?

There is no hierarchy of values listed in the Sermon on the Mount or among the works of mercy that says someone is more "blessed" than somebody else. And Jesus did not divide his teachings about justice and mercy into those appropriate for women and those appropriate for men. Even though women may have been socialized into thinking they were meant to be meek rather than seek justice, there is nothing in Jesus' teachings to support this. And there is nothing there to *excuse* them for being meek instead of seeking justice.

The very word *meek* causes problems for us. It connotes quite a few really separate concepts: patience, humility, long-suffering, submissiveness, spinelessness, kindness, and gentleness. Certainly not all the same thing. The word poses numerous questions for us.

Are we, for example, to be meek in the face of injustice?

Are only women to be meek? Is a woman whose husband beats her to suffer in silence? Must a woman be constantly self-effacing? Could it possibly mean that a *man* is called to be humble *rather than to humble others?* Could it possibly mean that gentleness and kindness are virtues equally desirable in men and women?

How do we decide what it means to be meek? It is a difficult question to answer when our sense of justice tells us the work we must be dedicated to is the work of empowering the powerless. At first, power and meekness seem to be in conflict.

A Christian finds it necessary to look for resolutions of conflict in the teachings of Jesus. And there we can learn from his example as well as from his sayings. What do we learn from him about meekness and about power? Whom did he require to be meek? Whom did he empower?

We know that Jesus cared for little children and for women. He certainly was not arrogant. Nor did he use his growing reputation to climb the social ladder of his society; instead, he used it to confront the hypocrisy of the power structure. He chose to spend time with some of society's outcasts. Yet he wasn't a reverse snob. He was demanding of the rich and powerful, but he did not automatically exclude them. He asked them instead to humble themselves for the poor.

Who can read Scripture with an open heart and seriously wonder whose side God is on in the movement to rid our society and our church of sexism?

2

With God on Their Side

There are feminists today who frankly have contempt for traditional religion. And some religious leaders have made it clear that the feeling is mutual.

But the wonder of the Christian religion is not that women did not reject it sooner. The wonder is that, despite the sexism that permeates religious history, independent female spirits continued to explode from time to time, proclaiming the truth and demanding justice within the context of being loyal Christian women. History has swallowed these women for the most part, but now feminist theologians and historians are rediscovering them for us.

Theologian Elisabeth Schussler Fiorenza urges us to rediscover Mary Magdalene, "indeed a liberated woman" whose life was radically transformed by her encounter with Jesus:

> According to all four gospels, Mary Magdalene is the primary witness for the fundamental data of the early Christian faith: she witnessed the life and death of Jesus, his burial and his resurrection. She was sent to the disciples to proclaim the Easter kerygma. Therefore Bernard of Clairvaux correctly calls her "apostle to the Apostles." Christian faith is based upon the witness and proclamation of women. As Mary Magdalene was sent to the disciples to proclaim the basic events of Christian faith, so women today may rediscover by contemplating her image the important function and role which they have for the Christian faith and community.

Yet, when we think of Mary Magdalene, we do not think of her first as a Christian apostle and evangelist; rather we have before our eyes the image of Mary as the sinner and the penitent woman. Modern novelists and theological interpreters picture her as having abandoned sexual pleasure and whoring for the pure and romantic love of Jesus the man. This distortion of her image signals deep distortion in the self-understanding of Christian women. If as women we should not have to reject the Christian faith and tradition, we have to reclaim women's contribution and role in it. We must free the image of Mary Magdalene from all distortions and recover her role as apostle. (From "Feminist Theology as a Critical Theology of Liberation," in *Woman: New Dimensions,* 1975).

Just as the "good news" on which the Christian faith is founded was first proclaimed by women, there seems to be an explosion today of women proclaiming a fuller message of the gospel to the church.

Consider Dr. Jeanette Piccard, who at the age of 79, when people were thinking of her as the venerable Dr. Piccard, fulfilled a lifelong ambition to become an Episcopal priest. She was already a woman of "achievement," having been the first woman in history to reach the stratosphere in 1934. She could have retired, but instead she joined the struggle for women's equality within the Episcopal Church, because since the age of 11 what she had really wanted to be was a priest.

She became one of the first 11 women irregularly ordained and later officially recognized by her church. Having achieved her dream, she continued until her death at the age of 82 to speak and inspire by her very presence her sisters and brothers who share her dream of equality, including Roman Catholic women working for ordination to the priesthood.

"To speak the truth with love" is the way Sister Theresa Kane describes the prophetic work of women within the church today. (Many would also choose those words to describe her historic 1979 greeting to the Pope in Washington D.C.) As the spokeswoman for the leaders of women's religious orders in the United States, Sister Theresa used her position to call the church to examine its conscience concerning women: "The church cannot profess dignity, reverence, and equality for all persons and continue to systematically exclude women as persons from fully participating in the institutional church," she said in a 1980 address in Philadelphia.

While the church preaches a message of "dignity, reverence and equality of all persons" throughout the world, Sister Kane maintained the church has not yet recognized the injustices it imposes on women. "Until the institutional Catholic Church undertakes a serious, critical examination of its modes of acting toward women, it cannot, it will not, give witness to justice in the world. The challenge for women in the '80s is to confront and eradicate the systemic evils of sexism, clericalism, and paternalism."

There are many other women and men also speaking the truth with love in the church today. Some of them have suffered and more will probably suffer for justice's sake— just as the prophets before them.

One such prophet, early on the shores of the New World, and now relegated to the footnotes of American history, was Anne Hutchinson.

Arriving in Boston in 1634, Anne Hutchinson found the Massachussetts Bay Colony to be a theocracy with a rigid

Calvinism that did not welcome her unorthodox beliefs that God existed in every human being and that individuals had direct communion with God. Colony officials were disturbed to learn that groups of 60 or more women and men were meeting at the Hutchinson home to listen to her theories—as well as to her criticism of the Calvinist ministers.

Since church and state were one in the Massachusetts Bay Colony, the officials feared that the entire community was being subverted. By asserting that individuals could have direct communion with God, Hutchinson was claiming equality of all citizens with the men who ruled the colony. This was heresy, and the authorities attacked her on religious and civil grounds. After an unfair trial in which she was not allowed to introduce evidence in her own defense, she was found guilty and banished from the colony. Excommunicated, she left the colony with only a woman named Mary Dyer publicly supporting her. Historian Eleanor Flexner records that Mary Dyer ". . . first roused to questioning by Mistress Hutchinson—would pay the price 22 years later when Boston's rulers, still hot for orthodoxy, hanged her as a Quaker."

Hutchinson and her family moved on to the new colony of Rhode Island, and four years later, when new theological disputes began to develop there, they moved into the wilderness of what is now Long Island, where they were killed by Indians as part of a land fraud dispute with the Dutch.

Eleanor Flexnor credits Anne Hutchinson with being the first person on the continent to challenge the place "habitually assigned to women in the new society then taking shape":

The ruthlessness of Anne Hutchinson's punishment is the

measure of her stature and her threat to the Puritan way of life and faith. Unschooled—save for her knowledge of the Bible—because she was a woman; inexperienced in rhetoric or debate—because she was a woman—she nevertheless won to her beliefs a large portion of a community highly conscious of theology. She challenged its best-educated, best-trained minds until they had to fall back on falsehood and compulsion.... (*Century of Struggle*, 1959)

As the life of Anne Hutchinson makes clear, religion and women's rights have been bound together from the beginning of our country just as they were in older patriarchal societies. Not only have women been kept in their place by the double agents of patriarchy and religion, but paradoxically, they have also continued to find in religion the seeds of their own sense of equality.

Jesus Seemed to Like Women

If Tertullian's third century opinion that woman was the gate of the devil were a truly Christian insight, we would never know it from Jesus. That attitude was alive and well during the time Jesus was teaching in Palestine, but he would have none of it. Unlike some of his male followers down through the centuries, Jesus actually seemed to *like* women.

When a woman reads the sayings of Jesus and reads about his actions in the four gospels of the New Testament, she does not get any sense of Jesus harboring male supremacist attitudes. Instead, she gets a sense that Jesus was a good friend to women. He seemed to ignore Jewish taboos and attitudes of superiority towards women; he treated women respectfully and kindly. They were among his close friends, and he seemed to be comfortably relaxed in their company.

Considering that Jesus often was explicit about what he expected of his followers, it seems important that he omitted from his teachings a reinforcement for the patriarchal order that requires women to submit to men. (This omission seems particularly significant in view of the fact that so many communities of latter-day Christians regard such order as a cornerstone of faith.)

What Jesus did reveal, however, was a concern that women be given justice. His teachings narrowed the grounds by which a man could divorce his wife. This teaching actually was a teaching of justice for women, as well as a teaching about the sacredness of marriage.

Similarly, women who read the gospels may feel a sense of relief that Jesus demanded justice for the woman accused of adultery. "Let the man among you who has no sin be the first to cast a stone at her," Jesus told the scribes and Pharisees who pointed out to him that the law of Moses required them to stone an adulteress. (John 8: 5-7)

When a woman reads such passages in the New Testament, it is not uncommon for her to experience a sense of Jesus as a liberated and *liberating* man whose words and actions affirm the equality of women and men that is essential to her. (For her own peace of mind, however, the woman should avoid *too frequently* delving into the words and actions of some of Jesus' disciples as recorded after his death in the epistles. These disciples discovered that Jesus was, as we now say, a tough act to follow—especially where women were concerned.)

Again and again throughout the gospels, Jesus rejects the injustices that resulted from following the letter of the law. He revealed a new spirit of the law, concerned for justice and compassionate love. By word and deed, he showed people that to follow him meant to stand with the weak and powerless. No wonder women were his close friends and eagerly followed him as he went about the country teaching.

Not only was Jesus friendly to women, however; he also assigned to women the responsibility for bearing witness to him—an unorthodox action in Jewish society because women were not accepted as witnesses. Most significantly, it was women to whom Jesus first appeared after his resurrection, telling them to go and notify the men. Women had stood by Jesus throughout his ordeal on the cross, and, unlike the male disciples, there is no record that the women ever denied him or deserted him.

So What Went Wrong?

Somewhere in the first century the liberating spirit that resulted in a conviction that in a Christian community there is neither Jew nor Greek, male nor female, slave nor free was subverted by old attitudes that reasserted the superiority of some people and the inferiority of others.

What went wrong is that sexism seeped into the new religion almost from the beginning. The followers of Jesus eventually were absorbed into a church that identified not only with the teachings of Jesus but also with the reigning power structure. And that power structure was controlled by males for the benefit of males. The power structure served the church, and the church served the power structure in a way not entirely unlike the pagan gods and the Roman emperors. As empires became more "holy," the church was frequently less so.

The church now recalls with shame that "followers of Jesus" were on hand with raised crosses to rationalize slavery. They were on hand to bless white men when native tribes were cheated, robbed, and annihilated. Routinely, they were on hand to bless all sorts of wars. And they have been on hand throughout most of church history to bless the subjugation of women to men.

It is really not a scandal that the followers of Jesus are sinners. That's the sort for which he was looking. The idea was supposed to be, however, that through him they would be saved from their sins. Fortunately, the teachings of Jesus include a generous allowance for sinners to repent, again and again, if necessary. How often must he forgive someone who wrongs him, the Apostle Peter wanted to know— seven times? "No," Jesus replied, "not seven times; I say, seventy times seven times." (Matthew 18: 21-22) The scandal is that the church does not repent of its sins but perpetuates and increases them by inventing more sins to rationalize its earlier ones. This is what the church has done to women. This is sexism.

Consider this excerpt from "The Woman Question," an article that appeared in 1869 in *The Catholic World,* a publication for educated Catholics, published in New York and illustrating the embarrassing fact that when women demanded the right to vote there were churchmen on hand to explain why this should never be allowed:

A certain number of women have become, in some way or other, very thoroughly convinced that women are deeply wronged, deprived of their just rights by men. . . . They claim to be in all things man's equal, and in many things his superior, and contend that society should make no distinction of sex in any of its civil and political arrangements. . . . The women in question claim for women all the prerogatives of men; we shall, therefore, take the liberty to disregard their privileges as women. They may expect from us civility, not gallantry. . . .

Suffrage and eligibility are not natural, indefeasible rights, but franchises or trusts conferred by civil society. . . . Ask you who constitute political society? They, be they more or fewer, who, by the actual constitution of the state, are the sovereign people. . . . In the United States, the sovereign people has hitherto been, save in a few localities, adult males of the white race, and these have the right to say whether they will or will not extend suffrage to the black and colored races, and to women and children. . . .

This disposes of the question of right, and shows that no injustice or wrong is done to women by their exclusion, and that no violence is done to the equal rights on which the American republic is founded. . . . We ask not if women are equal, inferior, or superior to men; for the two sexes are different, and between things different in kind there is no relation of equality or of inequality. Of course, we hold that the woman was made for the man, not the man for the woman, and that the husband is the head of the wife, even as Christ is the head of the church, not the wife of the husband. . . .

However, lest the reader get the wrong impression that the authors of this article did not like women, they hastened to add:

. . . We are Catholics, and the church has always held in high honor chaste, modest, and worthy women as matrons, widows, or virgins. Her calendar has a full proportion of female saints, whose names she proposes to the honor and veneration of all the faithful. . . .

Moreover, the authors said, in opposing political enfranchisement of women, they had the best interests of both men and women at heart. The "conclusive objection to the political enfranchisement of women is, that it would weaken and finally break up and destroy the Christian family." In words that echo through some Christian churches even in the closing decades of the 20th century, the 19th century authors complained:

> . . . We are daily losing the faith, the virtues, the habits, and the manners without which the family cannot be sustained; and when the family goes, the nation goes too or ceases to be worth preserving. . . . A large and influential class of women not only neglect but disdain the retired and simple domestic virtues, and scorn to be tied down to the modest but essential duties— the drudgery, they call it—of wives and mothers. This, coupled with the separate pecuniary interests of husband and wife secured, and the facility of divorce . . . allowed by the laws of most of the States of the Union, make the family, to a fearful extent, the mere shadow of what it was and of what it should be. . . .

> Woman was created to be a wife and a mother; that is her destiny. . . . For this she is endowed with patience, endurance, *passive* courage [emphasis added], quick sensibilities, a sympathetic nature, and great executive and administrative ability . . . [The] woman's rights party, by seeking to draw her away from the domestic sphere, where she is really great, noble, almost divine, and to throw her into the turmoil of political life, would rob her of her true dignity and worth. . . .

31

The more things change, the more they stay the same. Aware of this, more and more women are asking one another how they can continue to participate in sexist religions.

Is it surprising then that toward the end of her career and right up to the end of her life the great American suffrage leader Elizabeth Cady Stanton was primarily concerned about the role that established religion played in keeping women in an inferior position? In 1895, she began publishing volumes of The Woman's Bible, analyzing Old Testament passages harmful to women. Although other suffragists, fearing to alienate religious people, rejected association with her indictment of religion, Stanton continued writing until her death.

3

Sanctifying Sexism

It is easy to understand why 19th-century males resisted the efforts of women to enter the universities. The mystery is why men ever permitted women to learn to read in the first place. Sooner or later they were bound to stumble over Aristotle. And eventually, they would figure out just how much they owed to this giant thinker of ancient Greece.

The male, wrote Aristotle, "is by nature superior, and the female inferior; and the one rules, and the other is ruled."

And in yet another example of his genius, the philosopher explained the differences between man and woman more fully:

> The fact is, the nature of man is the most rounded off and complete, and consequently in man the qualities or capacities . . . are found in their perfection. Hence woman is more compassionate than man, more easily moved to tears, at the same time is more jealous, more querulous, more apt to scold and to strike.
>
> She is, furthermore, more prone to despondency and less hopeful than the man, more void of shame or self-respect, more false of speech, more deceptive, and of more retentive memory. She is also more wakeful, more shrinking, more difficult to rouse to action, and requires a smaller quantity of nutriment.

Fifteen hundred years later the seeds of misogyny planted by Aristotle's wisdom would flower throughout

Sanctifying Sexism

Christendom in the landmark theology and bizarre biology of St. Thomas Aquinas:

> As regards the individual nature, woman is defective and mis-begotten, for the active force in the male seed tends to the production of a perfect likeness in the masculine sex; while the production of woman comes from defect in the active force or from some material indisposition, or even from some external influence, such as that of a south wind, which is moist. . . .

And so it came to pass that Aristotle begot Aquinas, and Aquinas begot a lot of mischief. Amusing and ludicrous as their ideas of women now seem, we must not forget that their influence helped perpetuate injustice for women. The atrocities committed against women in the name of male-centered religion included such physical destruction as burning at the stake and the more universal destruction of women's autonomy—a situation which is the norm and not the exception.

Sexist theology served well a sexist society, sanctifying the lies on which the structure is based.

This is not what Jesus had in mind.

Subverting the Teachings of Jesus

In its beginning, Christianity was a liberating force for women. Here was this man Jesus teaching women, treating them with respect, telling them not to get hung up on their kitchen chores. In a culture in which women were virtually nothing, Jesus treated them matter-of-factly as human beings.

It's not surprising then that many women were among

his followers. And in the years after his death and resurrection, it's not surprising that many more women would be attracted to a Christian community by such ideas as expressed in St. Paul's letter to the Galatians 3: 28—"There does not exist among you Jew or Greek, slave or free, male or female. All are one in Christ Jesus."

But such hints of equality between sexes and classes were threatening to any male raised in a patriarchal climate, and it wasn't long before there were rumblings of discontent about Christian women. Paul's few words that formed his response to the conflicting spirits of Christianity and patriarchy during the first century have multiplied and echoed down through the centuries with a force unequaled by many of the teachings of Jesus himself. Paul struck a chord that males of the first century were as eager to hear as males of the 20th century. Some men, in fact, revere Paul's words as if they were the heart of the Christian message. Especially these words from the first letter to Timothy 2:11, an epistle that some scholars maintain Paul did not even author: "A woman must learn in silence and be completely submissive. I do not permit a woman to act as teacher or in any way to have authority over a man; she must be quiet." Can you imagine how relieved some males must have been when that letter was first read to them?

And if they liked that, they must have loved Paul's letter to the Ephesians 5: 22-24:

> Wives should be submissive to their husbands as if to the Lord because the husband is head of his wife just as Christ is head of his body the church, as well as its savior. As the church submits to Christ, so wives should submit to their husbands in everything.

35

How these words have thrilled men through the centuries!

There was nothing new in those teachings, and there was no explanation as to how they squared with the teaching that in Christ there was neither male nor female. Along with admonishing wives to be submissive to their husbands these same epistles contained admonishments to slaves to be submissive to their masters. And yet there was to be no slave or free in Christ. Perhaps, women and slaves had begun to believe too strongly in the liberating message of Jesus. The author of the epistles was acknowledging the overwhelming force of the patriarchal society in which Christianity began. From its beginning Christianity has had to allow for the human element of sinfulness operating within it. And here, among first century Christians was the sin of sexism beginning to cloud the truth of equality that Jesus had brought to women and men. The distortion of the "good news" had begun.

But even in this sexist climate women were doing important work in the church. They were ordained as deacons, just as men were, and they performed ministries that were catechetical, liturgical, sacramental, prophetic, or administrative.

Most scholars believe, however, that women were never ordained to the priesthood in the church, and church officials rely on this tradition for the basis of the continuing practice of excluding women from the church's priesthood. This tradition is especially important, since in 1976 the Pontifical Biblical Commission in Rome concluded that scriptural grounds alone are not enough to exclude the possibility of ordaining women priests—a conclusion Protestant Christians reached much earlier.

Others have pointed out that not only were women not ordained to the priesthood as we know it, but neither were men. The priesthood, as we know it, did not exist. The word "priesthood" referred to the priesthood of all believers.

As the hierarchical structure of the church evolved, however, women more and more were excluded from the upper echelons. A study commisioned by the U.S. bishops' Ad Hoc Committee for Women in Society and the Church concluded that there was a valid ordination of women to the diaconate at some periods during the first 600 years of Christianity, but women's role diminished after that for several reasons. It became more acceptable for men to minister to women, for one thing. And there may have been a need to distinguish Christianity from paganism, in which priestesses played a role, as well as to distinguish it from heretical sects which had women priests and bishops.

Sexism should not be discounted as a possible reason either.

British author Joan Morris has compiled a fascinating hidden history of women in the church with her book *The Lady Was a Bishop.* As an example, she described a mosaic and a marble slab in the Church of St. Praxedis in Rome. Both refer to a woman as "Theodora episcopa"—episcopa meaning bishop. The name on the mosaic has been tampered with and appears as "Theodo" (a male name) but the veiled head in the mosaic is that of a woman.

Morris also describes a fresco in the Cappella Greca of the Catacombs of Priscilla in Via Salerio Nova, Rome where some of the tombs date back to the first half of the second century. The fresco seems to show women concelebrating a eucharistic meal.

Much more work needs to be done to reclaim women's

history in the church if women and men hope to eliminate the accumulation of lies about their lives.

Theologian Rosemary Radford Ruether has demonstrated that, in addition to validating the sexism of the old patriarchal social structure, Christianity carried forth a misogyny from the Old Testament and developed a complicated "spiritual femininity." Both served to suppress any aspirations for equality that Christian women might have glimpsed in the teachings of Jesus.

The misogyny in the Judaeo-Christian tradition derives from the idea that Eve is the source of sin in the world. There is a continuation of this tradition of misogyny in the taboos that made women unclean and untouchable during menstruation. In Judaism women were forbidden to enter the inner sanctuary of the temple, and during menstruation they could not enter the outer courtyard either. Priests had to be free of all contact with women.

In addition to assimilating these attitudes from the Jews, early Christian thinkers also assimilated an element of Greek philosophy that contributed to the misogyny that developed along with the developing Christian theology.

The Greeks believed in a dualism of body and soul, with the soul being the superior part of human nature. This philosophy resulted in men being defined with the superior, God-like thinking capacity of human nature and women being identified with the so-called inferior, animalistic part of human nature. Naturally the body with its needs, especially its sexual needs, posed a constant problem for the spiritual nature of men. This was particularly true later in Christianity for men living lives of celibacy. Is it any wonder that as celibacy came to be a requirement for attaining power and making decisions in the Christian church, the exercise of power and the results of decisions carried overtones of this misogyny?

But Christianity offered women an important option that the ancient Greeks did not. They could become nuns. As nun, woman could also choose a celibate life and overcome her carnal female nature that ordinarily would have doomed her to her "natural" role in patriarchal society—the role of wife and mother, a life of toil and painful childbearing, over which the woman had no control and through which she was condemned forever to atone for the sin which the first woman, Eve, had brought to the race.

A nun, on the other hand, had a superior status. Abbesses in the Middle Ages had powers similar to bishops, with churches, villages, and priests under their administration. Some even heard confessions.

During the Renaissance period, the power of the quasi-episcopal abbesses began to wane. Monks under the rule of abbesses began to rebel on the basis that for man to be obedient to woman was contrary to nature and the will of God. Changes made by the Council of Trent resulted in the diminishment of the power of these independent women and brought them under the control of the church's male hierarchy. As Joan Morris writes:

It was only after the 12th century when there was a slow return to Greco-Roman culture reaching its zenith during the Renaissance that the services rendered by abbesses were looked upon as wrong. . . . The dislike of women having any right to rule shows that the whole idea of what it means to rule had become repaganized. Administration was no longer considered a service but a right of dominion, a right to lord it over another, which was the pagan idea of government and not the Christian one of humble service.

Whenever independent women have arisen in history there have been fearful men on hand to undermine them. Rosemary Ruether points out that even though nuns were women of superior status in the Christian church, another peculiar sort of dualism kept them from being the equals of any male celibate:

> Male virginity was defined as restoring the male to his "natural, spiritual virility," while the female virgin was described as "unnatural" having transcended her natural female nature and having become "unnaturally virile." To a large extent, these asymmetrical definitions of male and female attainments in the spiritual realm still define our culture, defining male cultural achievements as enhancing his masculinity while defining female intellectual achievements as rendering her unfeminine. (From "Sexism and Liberation: The Historical Experience," in *From Machismo To Mutuality,* 1976.)

Such theological gymnastics by men who taught in the name of Jesus of Nazareth might be laughable today were it not for the enormous repercussions such thinking has had on women's lives. Christians furthermore invoked the image of Jesus' mother, spotless virgin as well as mother, creating an impossible ideal of womanhood. In contrast, they had the sinful, sexual mother Eve. During the late Middle Ages, as Ruether observes, this two-woman concept intensified so that it finally "erupted in a veritable orgy of paranoia" that resulted in witch hunts that killed an estimated million or more women between the 14th and 17th centuries. It is no coincidence, she adds, that during this same period Mariology reached its greatest heights and triumphed with the doctrine of the Immaculate Conception.

Christian churchmen's complicity with the patriarchal power structure in inventing new reasons for women's inferior status eventually backfired, however. With the coming of the Industrial Revolution the concept of "dualism" reappeared to separate the private and the public spheres of human activity.

The power was in the public sphere with the decision makers. Religion became a function of the powerless private sphere of the home. The inhabitants of the public sphere were, of course, men. But since the inhabitants of the private sphere were women—previously thought to be inferior spiritually, bound as they were to bodily functions—it was necessary somehow to elevate women. The imaginary fantasyland called the pedestal was invented.

Somehow, after having been a basically unclean and corrupting influence on men, women supposedly became the moral superiors of men and the guardians of humankind's spiritual and religious values. Considering from where they had come, we can understand why many women willingly stepped onto this pedestal—not realizing as they did so that they were stepping sideways not upwards.

As usual, the bottom line was power. And men retained it:

Now the "real world" was the material world, the world of science, technology and technical rationality. Men became "more materialistic" and women "more spiritual" at precisely the moment when the material world became the "real world" from which power flowed, and the spiritual world became an atavistic realm of private sentimentality that no longer interpenetrated the realm of power. (From "Sexism and Liberation: The Historical Experience," in *From Machismo To Mutuality,* 1976.)

But finally Christianity itself paid the price for consorting with sexism. Having served a sexist power structure well, the church was ultimately cut out of real power. It still served a useful function, but now:

> The woman and the clergyman find themselves ensconced in the same golden cage and bidden to sing sweet songs of gentleness, love, mercy, and forgiveness that society reveres in its moments of private rectitude, but that it has no intention of allowing to interfere with the real business of running "the world." (Ibid.)

Sexist theology has long served well a sexist society, sanctifying lies on which the structure is based. This is not what Jesus had in mind for his followers.

Different Sex/Different Virtue

Although it has long been asserted that Christian churches have benefited women by raising their status, Christianity has been as infested with sexism as any human institution, and it has helped perpetuate sexism by coating it with sweet piety.

For example, there is the notion—still actively promoted in many communities—that man is the head of the home and woman is the heart of the home. An orderly, even cozy notion, to be sure. But in its orderly distinction between sexes, it conveys the insidious propaganda that decision making—the head work—had best be left to men. Women's world is properly the warm, cuddly preserve of the heart. And the hearth. For in the words of an idea that dies hard, "Woman is queen of the home." This lofty image defines woman's territory, her place, her limits.

Why should virtues be divided according to sex? Jesus made no separate lists of virtues for males and virtues for females. Yet Christians consciously or unconsciously have sometimes cooperated in the development of virtues based on sex.

In practice, women have been encouraged to develop and emphasize more passive virtues than men have. Women have been taught to be more humble than men, more oriented toward serving others. This passive orientation has been useful for the church itself and for the world outside the church. In addition to women's service-oriented obligations in their homes, affluent women are encouraged to donate their service to volunteer organizations rather than to seek paid employment. They are made to feel guilty if they earn money they "do not need." Women laborers are taught to feel guilty if they "take a job from a man"—the implication being that the man's job is necessary to support a family and the woman's is not.

How subtly all of this used to occur and how deeply it invaded the recesses of our spirits! This was brought home to me emphatically one day as I was dusting a bookshelf and came across a small black prayer book, *Woman Before God.* It had been a gift 15 years earlier from a college friend. Easily distracted from dusting, I opened the book to refresh my memory. By chance I had opened it to a page of tiny black type headed by one word in red: "Equality?"

". . . Those who preached rights to us forgot to tell us that the strength of a woman lies in her weakness and that service is her way of mastery," the page read. "The entire structure of our lives has been confused. That which is of our very nature—womanhood—is not to be found in the 'declaration of our rights.'

"A woman who is conscious of her real nature never doubts her rights. But because she is a woman, she is intelligent enough to remain silent on this matter. She has learned to serve and precisely in this has she become the guiding force of human destinies that she is."

Then followed a prayer, placed there I assume as reinforcement for the previous meditation on the sanctified inequality that the author called "equality." It read:

> Lord, my ideas cannot change the ways of society. Nor can I wish to live in a different age. I probably would not want to, even if you gave me the chance. But I pray you, O Lord, let me recognize from day to day that you have created mankind as man and woman. Let me understand that I am a woman. Give me insight into my own peculiar nature as woman. Let me, O Lord, not attempt to make something out of myself which you did not intend. Amen.

Another uplifting prayer followed immediately on the heels of the first:

> In the beginning of creation, O God, you said that the woman should be subject to the man; that he should be her master. This word of yours stirs up my pride to rebellion. Teach me to obey my husband so that, in obeying him, I may learn how to command. Amen.

There was no explanation at this point of how I might learn how to command by obeying, nor was there any explanation as to why someone 1) who did not wish to be something that God did not intend to create should 2) wish to learn to command, when 3) God intended her not to command. No, all there was was this quotation from Pope Pius XI's *Casti Connubii:* "If the man is the head of the family, the woman is the heart, and as he occupies the chief place in ruling, so she may and ought to claim for herself the chief place in love."

Love?

I thought I was reading about "Equality?"

Ah! See the subtle trick played on woman's weak head and oversized heart! If it is love that woman wants—and what human being does not want love?—then she ought not to challenge men with demands for equality.

There the page ended, and I turned it with trepidation as I felt welling up in me a sadness and sense of deja vu, faces of old friends, relatives, fading in my memory now, making choices based on love, following their hearts. As if to jolt me out of this, the next page was a masterful piece of propaganda. It was sincerely meant, no doubt, but it was propaganda still. It was a two-page spread with one page devoted entirely to a photo of a young woman contentedly cuddling a plump, bare-bottomed baby. Love. Yes, love. On the opposite page, printed with the look of an important declaration was this text:

The right to serve and to love,
  The right to sympathize,
The right to nurse the infant tenderly—
  To guide, teach, and warn,
The right to be awake when all are sound asleep,
  The right to bring light to darkness,

> The right to bear with patient love the burdens
>   and cares of others,
> The right to believe firmly and to remain
>   faithful, when fearful doubts surge,
>   The right to forgive without number,
> In a word—the right to be entirely woman,
>   full tender, good and true—
> That is the most beautiful of all woman-rights!

I did not remember ever having actually read this book before this, even when it was given to me. It had long been forgotten, but its words were familiar ones, familiar from my childhood and from various levels of religious indoctrination. They were also the words of current-day opponents of women's equality. While in today's words the author sounds more than a bit reactionary in his attitude toward women, in the early 1960s when this book was written, his attitude was a widely accepted one. Especially among Catholics for whom he wrote. I wondered how many messages such as this Christian women have unwittingly absorbed into their spirits only to find them poisoning their existence as the reality of life unfolds, or exploding into rage when they discover that they have unintentionally lived lives based on such lies. How often do these messages absorbed so long ago seep unconsciously into our actions just as this long-forgotten book showed up again in my life?

Professional women in the church have also been conditioned to develop passive virtues, leaving the more active ones to males. In the case of priests and nuns, for instance, both supposedly live lives dedicated to the same gospel, but they have traditionally been expected to live them very differently.

The nuns, often referred to patronizingly as the "good

sisters," have reserved to them the realm of love. Theirs is a virtue of service, of submission to authority, of educating children and caring for the old and sick, similar in many ways to mothers in the home. To priests are reserved the virtues of leadership, decision making, authority. Appropriately, they are referred to as "fathers." Nuns are counseled to cultivate the virtues of humility, selflessness, gentleness. Priests are thrust into positions in which they must struggle to keep their egos in balance—presiding at liturgies, preaching, counseling, forgiving sins, controlling lives.

Splitting virtue and life along sex lines in this way is no more valid for nuns and priests than it is for women and men in marriage. Human beings are male and female. Both are composed of head and heart, of rational and emotional capacity, of the ability to reason and the ability to feel. To assign one or the other function primarily to one sex or the other is to do injustice to both. Not only is the woman who is confined to the realm of the heart not given credit for her rational capacity, but she is unfairly asked to carry the emotional capacity of her male partner as well as herself. As for the man, an injustice is done to him as well. When he is assigned prime responsibility for the realm of the head, he is expected to deny his emotional self, and he is asked to assume a double burden of living a meaningful life himself and providing meaning for a woman's life. While this system understandably suits some men just fine, the large numbers of men who have broken under these expectations usually have their failure blamed on something else. Somewhere among the statistics of alcoholism, suicide, wife beating, desertion, and other sorrows that plague us are the stories of men who couldn't take the rigid definition of what it means to be a man.

Sanctifying Sexism

Fundamentalists and "God's Divine Plan"

The notion that it is God's eternal plan for men and women to be confined to separate spheres dies hard. There are many people who blame all of the world's problems on the fact that rigid role definition by sex has begun to break down. They have found many willing listeners for this message, too; for men and women together have suffered and continue to suffer the pains of change as they struggle to overcome sexism. For many, this transition has been a wrenching experience. They were dragged kicking and screaming into the stream of change and were confronted bitterly with it by being divorced or by divorcing the marital partner unwilling to change. Those men and women who confronted sexism as an injustice and began to grope together to evolve a more just way of living together, simply do not attract the attention that our alarming divorce statistics do. At the beginning of the 1980s, one out of three American marriages ended in divorce.

And so there is a climate created in which a frightened constituency buys into the message that women have set nature off balance and are consequently responsible for a long list of weaknesses in every American institution from the family to the armed forces. If only, we are told, women would act like women, everything would be better.

There is something familiar about this refrain. It is a modern-day version of The Fall, with the liberated woman as Eve, responsible again for the fall of the human race. This ancient story echoes in the rhetoric of today's political and religious arch-conservatives. It was the theme behind the silly and truly pathetic outburst during the '70s of the Total Woman Movement—actually numerous courses offered to women under various names, but none of them better known than *The Total Woman,* a book and a training course of the same name by Marabel Morgan. Morgan and her many imitators offered their philosophy of pleasing and manipulating men as an antidote to the feminist movement.

In one such course, given in churches, women learned:

● To obey their husbands and be an example of how all people should submit to God;

● To return to their husbands, thereby leading the way for the rest of the human race to return to God;

● To adapt and yield to their husbands' decisions, but not to make their own decisions;

● To learn submission so that their husbands might learn what it really means to love.

Women frightened by the consequences of change that they saw all around them, frightened by the responsibility of having to make choices for themselves and risk having to blame only themselves for their failures, opted for security and desperately tried to accept that philosophy. Among them was singer Anita Bryant, who publicly crusaded for traditional family virtues under the direction of her husband Bob Green. Green incorporated as Anita Bryant Ministries and pushed his wife into a hate-producing crusade against homosexuals. But finally the lie upon which this so-called Christian ministry was built collapsed of its own weight when Bryant realized how she was being manipulated and used by Green and others. Anita Bryant is now divorced from Bob Green and presumably is a wiser woman for her experience.

"Fundamentalists have their head in the sand," she told an interviewer after her divorce. "The church is sick right now, and I have to say I'm even part of that sickness. Some pastors are so hard-nosed about submission and insensitive to their wives' needs that they don't recognize the frustration—even hatred—within their own households. Some of them are going to be shocked to wind up in my boat."

The most insidious, objectionable part of the reactionary Total Woman movement is its religious dimension. Too often churches have met the troubled soul searching of their women members by offering them the scriptural equivalent of Total Woman in Bible-quoting courses aimed at convincing the women that God's eternal plan is that for all time women are to be submissive to men. This reinforcement of ancient sexism flourishes now among Protestant fundamentalists, Catholic traditionalists, Mormons, charismatics, and followers of uncounted freelance preachers.

Some of this is understandable. Women, conditioned throughout history to look to men for direction, for answers, for authority, for their very definition of who they are, find it safer to grab onto this reassuring, traditional message than to face the choice of deciding for themselves who they are and how they will live their own lives. Instead of being "total" women, they are subtotal women—less than they were meant to be. Religion for them is Valium. But religion used in this way has become a tool for political backlash.

Christianity—A Tool for Backlash

The women's movement has fueled the Christian backlash movement by striking fear of change into the hearts of many men and confusion into the heads of their wives. Because of the women's movement, these people have glimpsed the truth of their lives, and it has been a painful glimpse. How comforting to go to the Bible and to hear a preacher provide a scriptural balm for the lie which the truth threatens to unmask. For 2,000 years, preachers have been defending patriarchy and claiming to defend Jesus' teaching. Their message is basically the same whatever their denomination: Wives be submissive to your husbands. Salvation will follow. Amen.

Once again in history we are witnesses to powerful men using Christian religion as a means of putting woman in her place. And her place, as they see it, is wherever there is no power. When they say a woman's place is in the home what they really mean is that it is in the home, in the typing pool, in the lower-paid professions, in the tomato fields, in the university housekeeping service, in the school cafeteria, on the minimum-wage assembly line. If woman's place really were in the home, our economy would grind to a halt. Women account for 42.8 percent of the U.S. labor force, and most of them are concentrated in the lowest paying jobs.

A Christian backlash, far from restoring woman to some mythical higher place, is involved in a manipulation of women's rights for political ends. Right-wing Christians and conservative political strategists have exaggerated fears and doubts about the Equal Rights Amendment and effectively linked it to a general malaise in the electorate that they blame on moral disorder in the family and society. They have also drawn into their camp many persons sincerely concerned about unrestricted abortions. Legitimate concerns and doubts of women are being manipulated in the quest for political power.

Not everyone who is a member of theologically conservative churches believes the antiwoman messages that are part of ultraconservative political strategies. Besides the highly publicized case of Sonia Johnson, the Virginia woman who was excommunicated by the Mormon Church because of her pro-ERA activity, there are numerous people who describe themselves as evangelical feminists. They are conservative theologically, relying on the Bible as their authority, but believing in a feminism that grows from the teachings of Jesus.

One such evangelical feminist learned the hard way how political objectives are infiltrating religious communities. Patricia Gundry wrote a book about biblical feminism, and her husband, who had been a teacher at Moody Bible Institute for 11 years, lost his job. Moody is located in Illinois, a state that has been the focus of exhausting battles for ratification of the ERA.

"It's a political situation caused by Stop-ERA activists conducting a smear campaign based on slander, innuendo, and distortion directed at Moody Bible Institute in order to get them to take a political stand against ERA," Ms. Gundry said. "The explanation is money and power." She believes Stop-ERA people promoted a campaign to get people to write to Moody complaining about the school having a teacher with a wife like her. The school acknowledges that the Gundrys' opinions about the feminist movement are objectionable to them and are the reason for the forced resignation.

Power, of course, is the blood of a political system, and in itself it is not objectionable. What is objectionable is braiding purely pragmatic political strategies with religious convictions. Our system has been suspicious of that from the beginning of our nation.

In the early 1970s, a liberal Presbyterian pastor with a passion for political organization wrote a book called *The*

Sleeping Giant. The giant was the church, which he viewed as scattered groups of people of various denominations, all of them slumbering and ineffective. He wanted to rouse this giant from its sleep, to call it to live up to the Christian principles it claimed to possess. It would be, he thought, a potent force for social justice in America. A decade later it looks as if a very different sort of giant awoke.

The Christian Voice, a conservative political action group organized before the 1980 election, claimed to have a constituency of 40 million "born-again" Protestants, 30 million conservative Catholics, and several million Mormons and Orthodox Jews that could be mobilized to support conservative candidates and issues that reflect "Christian moral implications." Christian Voice was just one of the vehicles by which religious conservatives' votes and dollars were solicited successfully for the 1980 political elections, resulting in a conservative sweep.

"It's a moral imperative for Christians to become active politically," said Christian Voice's legislative director Gary Jarmin, announcing his intention to mobilize fundamentalists. "The message that Christ left us was to occupy until he comes, and he didn't mean just the pews." (Such an observation amounted to advocating that Protestant fundamentalists do what anti-Catholic bigots used to accuse "papists" of plotting to do should they ever succeed in electing a president. John Kennedy disappointed them in this respect.)

Masterminding much of the conservative organizing was direct-mail entrepreneur Richard Viguerie who has built himself a $15 million a year business promoting conservative politics. The heart of his business and political strategy is his computerized direct-mail operation.

Viguerie and others, such as those behind Christian Voice, have shrewdly taken advantage of the sleeping giant of evangelical Christianity and the frustration and anger that many other Americans have about political issues. Evangelical Christians even have their own television and radio network. That network plus the church services and prayer meetings facilitate organizing. Television preachers such as Oral Roberts, Jerry Falwell, and Pat Robertson reach, by one estimate, 128 million viewers, increasing the influence of their religio-political ideas.

Phyllis Schlafly, the intrepid ERA opponent, is among those ultraconservative politicians who contributed to the coalition of conservative ideologies that achieved such remarkable success in 1980. And she is a good example of the cynicism that is necessary when attempting to sell a full range of conservative and right-wing conservative ideas with a pitch for God at the same time. Schlafly, whose political roots are closer to the John Birch Society, than to the pro-life movement, is an attractive, articulate Catholic woman who has drawn other Catholic women to her Stop-ERA banner because of her argument that the ERA would be advantageous for legalized abortion. She personally had no difficulty, however, when it came to endorsing an Illinois political candidate who opposed the ERA but voted against the pro-life measures.

For politicians, manipulating the fundamentalist religious believers in this way is merely a matter of a smart and effective use of modern communication techniques to identify and mobilize a power base. It is a political strategy that their opponents might even duplicate if they could.

But it is a different matter for the believers. Their duty

to God and to their political beliefs sometimes results in making a virtue of intolerance. It is a dangerous situation for a pluralistic country.

This Christian backlash is not the first of its sort to have an impact on women's rights in the United States. Clergy of an earlier day also made themselves available to advocate the status quo, and Catholics in particular remember their prominent cardinals who encouraged the backlash anti-suffrage movement when women were seeking the right to vote. In 1920, the *New York World* printed a report of Boston's Cardinal William O'Connell's vigorous condemnation of "sinister feminism." It was creating disorder throughout society, he charged:

> The one thing that will preserve proper order in your house is the Christian authority of the Christian father of a family. ... There is no doubt that one of the main causes of this sinister feminism, of which we read so much and see quite enough, is what would appear to be a growing weakness on the part of the manhood of the Nation.

> The very fact that women are so often clamoring to take all power and authority into their hands is certainly no compliment to the manhood of the Nation. ...

> After all, women, the wife and the children, expect a father to have and to exercise the rightful authority due to his position. But if he abdicates that position, if he has no love for his home, if he is away from it whenever he can be, if he takes no interest in the children except merely to give enough money to support them—well, no one can be surprised if, little by little, women learn to do without the authority of man and begin to usurp a great deal of it themselves.

That leads to a false feminism which certainly, unless it is curbed in time, will have disastrous results for humanity, because it is unnatural. . . .

The women are becoming masculine, if you please, and the men are becoming effeminate. This is disorder. . . .

We have another more recent example of religious backlash, however. In Iran, in 1979, when the westernized Shah was forced off his throne and the Ayatollah Ruhollah Khomeini proclaimed a theocracy called an Islamic Republic, one of the first items of business was an order that women in this Muslim country should resume the chador, which veiled them from head to toe. The Ayatollah furthermore wanted to suspend the Family Protection Law, which made what seem to us small changes in domestic law. But for Iranians the law made enormous changes: Women were permitted to divorce their husbands under a greater variety of circumstances, and men had to show cause when divorcing their wives; the permissible age of marriage was raised to 18 for women, although under some circumstances 15 was permitted. The Shah had instituted the law over the opposition of the clergy. Although, as in the early teachings of Christianity, there were elements of equality for women in the principles of Islam, the principles were overcome long ago by patriarchal practices. Despite the existence of many educated women, a woman in Iran today is still regarded as needing protection and separation from male predators, and her greatest purpose is to produce a son. In this respect she is linked to her sisters throughout the world. The differences are largely a matter of degree.

The patriarchal influence is more ancient than Islam, Christianity, or even Judaism.

It is interesting to note that close to the time the Ayatollah was implementing actions to put women in what he saw as their orderly place, there was a new pope in Rome doing something similar—though in a gentler, more subtle way. John Paul II, who became pope during a tumultuous time of international crisis, found himself pestered by a feminist element in the church, as well. In the United States, the movement to ordain women to the priesthood was receiving considerable publicity, and the women, including many U.S. nuns, had begun to organize and challenge the institutional church in ways uncomfortably similar to secular feminist challenges in society. The Pope's response to this ferment was to remind nuns of the importance of wearing religious garb of some sort and to remind other women of the pre-eminence of their roles as mothers. His early response to women, many felt, indicated a good and educated man who had no real understanding of women's situation in the world and who carried an idealized, but distorted, image of womanhood with him. He spoke to women not angrily, but often it seemed caringly, in a fatherly sort of way. And because of the very separate sort of life he has lived from the Catholic feminists he hopes to reason with, it would seem to be difficult indeed for him to understand that such fatherly advice reaches women's ears amplified as patriarchal repression.

In a fatherly way, the Pope urges women to find the role assigned to them in the church. Here and there commissions are established, reports are written, books are published, speeches are made, and arguments stalemate on "the role of women in the church." Again, this time in the 20th century, the role of women in the church is up for discussion. Women have been on earth as long as men. They have belonged to the Christian church as long as men. Where are the commissions to study the role of *men* in the church? Why is it the role of women that seems never to be settled? A step forward triggers a backlash and a step backward.

Contrary to those who believe that a divine spirit guides such backlash, there are many Christian men and women who believe that it is guided rather by the deeply rooted sin of sexism, more ancient than any of the great religions of the world. That this backlash is so powerful whenever it appears is evidence of the power of evil, not of God.

Why has this evil continued to be challenged? Why has this woman or that woman throughout history struggled to be free of sexism? This persistence is the real evidence of a divine spirit in human history, a spirit moving all people toward the truth.

Often the church pays lip service to its mission to "be against the world" not a part of it. But where women are concerned it often has not been true to this vocation. It has usually stood with the prevailing patriarchal view of women. It has stood, and in its official actions continues to stand, not against but *with* most of the world in support of the status quo for women.

4

Sexism's Not *My* Problem

You see it in their indulgent smiles, their eyes rolled impatiently while their lips are patiently silent.

Sure, they will tell you, if you press them on it, there is plenty of inequality in our lives. Yes, it's wrong; but no, I'm not going to spend time trying to change things. There are simply more urgent needs in the world today. Look, people are a) starving to death in Africa, b) being poisoned to death by industrial waste, c) on the verge of extinction thanks to nuclear bombs. You think I'm going to get excited about a petty rule that says my daughter can't be an altar boy? I'd rather she become a lawyer anyway.

Or, they put it this way: You may be right, but my first responsibility is to my family. I like what I'm doing. I love my family and my home. I enjoy being free to volunteer at church and help out at my kids' school. I really don't feel discriminated against. In fact, I'm pretty happy. So don't come along and ruin it.

Although their lives are based on it, sexism is simply not part of the vocabulary for many women. And eliminating sexism is not among their priorities in life.

The Last Shall Be First, Etc.

The traditional Christian woman has been conditioned by humility to suppress thought of herself. She has learned from the gospel that the first shall be last and the last shall be first. Both as a woman and as a Christian, she regards it as natural to defer to others, so serve, to think of herself last, to cut larger pieces of pie for her husband and sons. It is so ingrained a behavior that it seems to be part of her nature.

Because of this, it is not surprising that so many women do not put sexism high on their list of concerns. Or to put it another way, they do not see that striving for equality for themselves and for other women should take priority over the needs of others. There are always "more serious" things to be done first. Women's own needs come last. Didn't Jesus himself say "The last shall be first and the first shall be last"? (Matthew 20: 16)

That Jesus intended this instruction for all, not just for women, is forgotten by those who reason this way. There is nothing essentially Christian about the way women seem to naturally defer to men, whether at a meeting or during a decision about where a family will live and work. Rather, such deference is simple sex role conditioning, a universal human practice that predates Christianity and a practice that has been mortar for the sexist structures built by men, not God.

Promised a Pedestal

Supposedly there are rewards for women under this system, even though it is so obviously weighted to the advantage of the males they serve. Woman, we are to believe, is placed on a pedestal. She is above the coarseness of the business world, too good for politics, above dirty work. Woman—if she is a "good girl" and behaves in a "feminine" manner—is promised this special privilege.

In 1915, we had the word of Cardinal James Gibbons, of Baltimore, that women belonged on pedestals, and that men had women's best interests at heart in denying them access to the ballot box:

> Equal rights do not imply that both sexes should engage promiscuously in the same pursuits, but that each should discharge those duties which are adapted to its physical constitution. The insistence on a right of participation in active political life is undoubtedly calculated to rob woman of all that is amiable and gentle, tender and attractive; to rob her of her grace of character and give her nothing in return but masculine boldness and effrontery. Its advocates are habitually preaching about woman's rights and prerogatives, and have not a word to say about her duties and responsibilities. They withdraw her from those obligations which properly belong to her sex and fill her with ambition to usurp positions for which neither God nor nature ever intended her.

> When I deprecate female suffrage I am pleading for the dignity of woman. I am contending for her honor, I am striving to perpetuate those peerless prerogatives inherent in her sex, those charms and graces which exalt womankind and make her the ornament and coveted companion of man. Woman is queen indeed, but her empire is the domestic kingdom. The greatest political triumphs she would achieve in public life fade into insignificance compared with the serene glory which radiates from the domestic shrine and which she illumines and warms by her conjugal and motherly virtues. If she is ambitious of the dual empire of public and private life, then like the fabled dog beholding his image in the water, she will lose both, she will fall from the lofty pedestal where nature and Christianity have placed her and will fail to grasp the sceptre of political authority from the strong hand of her male competitor. . . .

Sexism's Not *My* Problem

The Cardinal was hardly the first man to use the image of a dog to describe a woman who did not "know her place," and in his romantic prose about the domestic kingdom there is a hint of what awaits a woman who ventures past the kingdom's border.

Ineligible for Pedestals—Bad Girls,
Poor Girls, and Independent Women

The notion of women being on pedestals seems to be something of a perversion of the Christian attitude that the last shall be first—in this case even *before* they get to the gates of heaven, as was promised in the gospel.

Of course a major problem with the Pedestal Theory, as well as with the Christian Pedestal Theory (that woman was downtrodden because of Eve, and *Jesus* raised her to a pedestal) is that so many members of womankind are ineligible for pedestals.

It goes without saying that bad girls are ineligible, because by definition, being on a pedestal implies feminine virtue. Prostitutes certainly are not eligible for pedestals. Actually only virgins of fine character, married women who behave themselves, and widows of certain virtue are eligible for pedestals.

Not even all of the "good girls" are eligible for pedestals. Poor women, no matter how fine their character, are certainly on no pedestals. They are needed to perform monotonous tasks on assembly lines for minimum wages, separated from other women who have been elevated to curious corporate pedestals and named secretaries. Poor women are needed to clean offices at night and do the dirty work in hospitals. If these women were permitted to occupy pedestals, who would do their work?

62

Also not eligible for the pedestal is the independent woman. Curiously, she is sometimes referred to as an "uppity woman" when she has deliberately declined to be elevated to a pedestal. "Women's libber," "castrater,"—the list of names for the independent woman seems to grow longer and more vicious. The woman who will not stay in her traditional place, the independent woman who choses to define for herself who she is and why she is—this woman not only is not respected, but she is increasingly debased.

It is a telling sign that male magazines which trade in exploitation of the female anatomy show an interest these days in displaying nude photos of allegedly liberated women. How a woman can call herself liberated and then reduce herself to a sex object is downright confusing. But there is nothing confusing about the instinct in some males to reduce the independent woman to a position of subjugation where she is serving men's needs, a woman's proper place.

Early on in the current wave of feminism there were people who liked to joke about the "unfeminine," "butch," or plain sloppy appearance that they attributed to angry feminist demonstrators on television. The implication in many of the remarks they made was that these were bitter women, not attractive enough to get husbands and determined to spread their misery. Men, in particular, could not understand how women could contemplate living without them. Some feminists responded to them with a slogan printed on t-shirts and posters: "A woman without a man is like a fish without a bicycle."

With that earlier distortion discredited, we now have male pornographers and magazine impresarios who take special delight in writing about the careers and "liberated" ideas of this playmate or that. They are just keeping up with the times and at the same time trying to still keep women in their place.

Women of Privilege

At certain points in our lives we experience special moments when the scales fall from our eyes and we see something clearly for the first time. We call these occasions moments of truth. One such moment in my life was the result of purchasing a brown suede skirt.

It was one of the best bargains I had ever found during January clearance days. I could hardly believe my good luck—a $75 suede skirt marked down to $25. And there was a whole rack of them, all sizes, all priced the same. I resisted a greedy urge to buy two and proudly took my bargain home.

Two years later I researched and wrote an article about the brutal repression of the free labor union movement among Korean women who worked long hours for miserable pay in a textile factory. A day or so after completing the article I happened to take my bargain suede skirt out of the closet. I noticed for the first time the skirt's label. It said only "Republic of Korea."

That was *my* moment of truth.

It was the moment at which I realized that as a privileged American consumer I also played a role in the exploitation of young women workers on the other side of the world. The store in which I had purchased my "bargain" could well afford to sell me the skirt at that price without taking a loss, because it was routinely charging excessively high prices for the clothes it sold while buying them dirt cheap from Korea, the Philippines, Mexico, Malaysia, and wherever workers—preferably young, female and docile workers—exist in vast, unorganized poverty. I stopped bragging about my "great buy" from that moment on.

The privileges some women enjoy are frequently based on the poverty of other women, and those privileged women who believe they were born to perch on a pedestal should know that their pedestals rest on the backs of other women they cannot see.

At the turn of the century it was the Irish immigrant maid who supported the gilded pedestals of privileged ladies by polishing silver and dusting chandeliers. And it was the German farm girl who sewed in the sweatshop owned by the ladies' husbands, helping to make the men rich enough to support wives on pedestals.

Today we look for support for our pedestals in the textile mills of Asia where our clothes are sewn or in the border towns of Mexico where cheap domestic help is available to help us care for homes that are too big for us in the first place. Those of us whose grandmothers were the Irish maids or the German sewing machine operators ought to know better. Our superiority requires someone else to be inferior.

In the early days of industrialization of our own country there was an exploitation of young women workers similar to that now going on in developing nations today. In the mid-1800s women working in cotton and woolen mills worked 12- to 16-hour days, earning only $1 to $3 a week, from which they had to pay $1.50 or more for shelter in company boarding houses.

By 1850, there were almost a quarter of a million women working in U.S. manufacturing—24 percent of the manufacturing labor force. They were an important factor in an expanding economy, and there was no talk of erecting domestic pedestals for them. They were unorganized, and efforts to unite them into a union had no lasting success until much later.

Among the women of privilege at that time were the middle-class women who built the women's rights movement, but for the most part they too did not grasp the relationship between the laboring women and the cause of women's rights until much later.

A fascinating glimpse into the mind of educated churchmen of the time is contained in an article called "The Woman Question," published in 1869 in *The Catholic World*. The article has 12 pages explaining that women should not be able to vote because they would neglect their families and bring disorder to the domestic sphere. There is a flourish of enthusiasm, too, for "conventual schools" then just being established and for the "modest, retiring sisters and nuns, who have no new theories or schemes of social reform" but are working to "raise woman to her true dignity." As an afterthought, there is a last paragraph tacked onto this middle-class vision for the church, an off-hand acknowledgment that even in 1869 there were not enough pedestals to go around. Wrote the anonymous author:

> For poor working-women and poor working-men, obliged to subsist by their labor, and who can find no employment, we feel a deep sympathy, and would favor any feasible method of relieving them with our best efforts. But why cannot American girls find employment as well as Irish and German girls, who are employed almost as soon as they touch our shores, and at liberal wages? There is always work enough to be done if women are qualified to do it, and are not above doing it. But be that as it may, the remedy is not political, and must be found, if found at all, elsewhere than in suffrage and eligibility.

About a hundred years later when the next wave of feminism had begun, there were many who accused the new feminists of also being upper-middle-class, white, professionally oriented, and estranged from the working class, minorities, and the poor. While there certainly are feminists who fit that description, the women's movement has struggled to be inclusive and reach across divisions of race and class. But there is so much more to do.

Women who want justice for women are realizing that their hunger for justice must cross borders and oceans. They must learn how U.S.-owned corporations are exploiting women and girls in poor countries and how privileged Americans are profiting from this directly, as owners, managers, or financiers, or indirectly, as consumers. (Some U.S. labor union members are aware of how they are *not* profiting from this situation as jobs go "off shore" to where there are no union wages.)

Privileged Americans who check their clothes, shoes, toys, and other "bargains" will discover "Made in Korea," or "Made in the Philippines," or "Made in Mexico" again and again. The reason is simple: U.S. assembly-line workers earn as much in an hour as some female workers in Third World nations earn in a day.

Furthermore there are no pesky restrictions on our corporations abroad, no bothersome demands about the health and safety of workers that cut into profits. It has been estimated that 80 to 90 percent of the assembly-line jobs that go to the Third World are performed by females, who can legally be paid less than men in such places. The preference is for uneducated, docile, single, teenage girls. Often they are over-the-hill at 30, their health ruined, and, in the case of the young women who use microscopes all day in U.S.-owned electronics plants, their eyesight ruined.

When such young women do attempt to organize for more pay or shorter hours, their own governments are on the side of management. In Korea, for example, when women at the Dong-Il Textile Company in Inchon gained leadership in their own union, male union members and company management collaborated in quashing their independence. They called upon a goon-squad that, among other things, smeared human excrement over the women's bodies and in their eyes, ears, and mouths. Government police stood by and did nothing.

The Dong Il workers, typical of other laborers in Korea, were making about $60 a month at the time. "On their books they say they're working an eight-hour day, though they're actually working these people 12 to 16 hours a day, and they just get their regular eight-hour pay," said an American missionary priest who has tried to help the women's union. "They say they have to do this in order to 'up' exports."

What happened at Dong Il is just one example of how South Korean and other Third World businessmen (often educated in American universities), in conjunction with authoritarian governments and U.S. corporations, are violating human rights to keep a tight control on profits.

Workers who attempt to stand up for their rights know they do so at great risk. At Dong Il, the young women staged protests and a hunger strike. When they did return to work, they were told to sign pledges that they would no longer associate with Christian labor organizations. When 123 women refused to sign the statement, they were fired. Their names and photographs were circulated to factories throughout the country, blacklisting them. Other labor organizers in Korea have reported being tortured by police who arrest them during peaceful demonstrations.

(It is worth noting that while Christianity is sometimes accused of being the enemy of women's rights, in Korea some Christian laypersons, ministers, and priests are in the forefront of the struggle for human rights, including the rights of women workers to a just wage and just working conditions.)

In a special report on the exploitation of these women in developing nations, Barbara Ehrenreich and Annette Fuentes, writing in the January 1981 *Ms.* magazine, estimated that as many as six million women may already have been "used up" and cast off in this way.

"As if poor health and the stress of factory life weren't enough to drive women into early retirement, management actually encourages a high turnover in many industries," they wrote. " 'As you know, when seniority rises, wages rise,' the management consultant to U.S. multinationals told us. He explained that it's cheaper to train a fresh supply of teenagers than to pay experienced women higher wages. 'Older' women, aged 23 or 24, are likely to be laid off and not rehired. . . . Few 'retire' with any transferable skills or savings. The lucky ones find husbands." The unlucky ones may be eventually forced into prostitution to support themselves.

Individuals in the business class in various countries do indeed grow rich along with their American counterparts in this global system, but the countries themselves do not benefit in the long run from the sacrifice of young women. As a United Nations representative of one of these countries told Ehrenreich and Fuentes:

"The multinationals like to say they're contributing to development, but they come into our countries for one thing— cheap labor. If the labor stops being so cheap, they can move on. So how can you call that development? It depends on the people being poor and staying poor."

It begins to grow clearer how businessmen in such economic arrangements come to rely on authoritarian governments to keep the natives from being restless.

And it begins to grow clearer that women who want justice must want it for women across the border and across the ocean as well as for themselves. We must learn to see the connection between the affluent lives we enjoy as privileged women and the denial of justice to other women. Unless middle-class feminists work for justice for these other women, along with justice for themselves, they are in danger of constructing for themselves a feminist pedestal that will be as dead an end for them as the other pedestal they have tried to avoid.

Women Against the ERA

There are many women in this country who do not share in the feminist agenda for justice. Many of these are women known and respected in the towns or neighborhoods for their many kindnesses to others. They take time during the week to deliver meals and friendship to elderly shut-ins. They are available to help when neighbors have illness or death in the family. They give money to charity, and often they go door to door collecting money from their neighbors for this cause or other. But if these women do not yet have a sense of the justice that is overdue for other members of their sex, then they are managing not to see the people who clean their hotel rooms or type letters in their offices or pick their tomatoes. Or the women who used to live in their neighborhoods before their husbands divorced them.

In the beginning of this century, it was privileged women who opposed women's suffrage—the issue of justice for women that stirred great controversy at the time. Now it is similarly privileged women who are opposing the Equal Rights Amendment to the U.S. Constitution.

The ERA is a short, simple statement of equality that was first proposed in 1923 by suffrage leader Alice Paul. For almost 50 years it was bottled up in committee by congressmen, but in 1972 it was finally approved by both houses of congress and sent to the states to be ratified. In 1978 with ratification stalled, Congress approved an extension of the ratification deadline until 1982.

All that the ERA says is this:

Section 1. Equality of rights under the law shall not be denied or abridged by the United States or by any state on account of sex.

Section 2. The Congress shall have the power to enforce, by appropriate legislation, the provisions of this article.

Section 3. This amendment shall take effect two years after the date of ratification.

Yet this simple statement of equality has become the battle ground on which the people who defend the traditional relationship of woman to man have chosen to defend that relationship against people who believe that justice requires change. ERA opponents accuse these few words of threatening everything from unisex toilets to the elimination of protective labor legislation for women. Ironically, it was conditions similar to what Third World factory women now experience that finally created public support in the U.S. to limit the long hours and inhuman conditions under which women and children worked in the 19th century.

Then protective legislation was an increase in the rights of working women; now it is being used as a threat to limit women's rights.

Phyllis Schlafly who has used her campaign against the ERA as a vehicle for her own right-wing conservative politics, summarizes what is wrong with ERA as a "big grab for vast new federal power." Laws governing marriage, property, inheritance, divorce, child custody, prisons, labor legislation, insurance rates, and abortion, she says, are better left in the hands of the states. She says this despite evidence that many such state laws are blatantly unjust to women. While Schlafly and her followers tell women that the states will protect their privileged standing as women, they shut their eyes to the women who have suffered under these laws, based as most of them are on the assumption of unequal contribution to marriage.

Curiously, while Schlafly would prefer to see states retain the right to regulate abortion, she has managed to generate a following among people whose number one political priority is to regulate abortion nation-wide by enacting a Human Life Amendment to the U.S. Constitution. Some of those who support a Human Life Amendment also support the ERA and oppose virtually everything for which Schlafly stands. Politics does indeed make strange bedfellows.

Schlafly's arguments do appeal to that element in the U.S. which has always favored the pre-eminence of states' rights over federal action. A war was once fought over this. Things are better left to the state legislatures, Schlafly says, and we note that many of those state legislatures which have so far agreed with Schlafly by refusing to ratify the ERA bear a striking geographic resemblance to the state legislatures that refused to ratify the 19th Amendment which gave women the right to vote—with the exception of the western states that have not ratified ERA but did support suffrage for women.

Schlafly, a mother of six children and wife of a lawyer, and law school graduate herself, has lived a comfortable, even affluent life. She is by any definition a privileged woman, and she has attracted to her cause many other similarly privileged women, effectively helping the right-wing network to which she has been connected throughout her long political career. She and her organization, Stop-ERA, have been helpful in exploiting the Christian backlash, providing testimony to support the theory that the nation's moral fiber is disintegrating and the women's movement is to be blamed. They have truly been women against women.

One disappointment of significance to Christian feminists has been the participation in the anti-ERA movement by some leaders and some local members of the National Council of Catholic Women, a network of parish women's groups which claims to represent 10 million women thoughout the country. Persuaded by arguments that ERA would harm the family and especially concerned that it might expand the legal basis for abortion, the NCCW has held fast in its long opposition to ERA.

This opposition has helped persuade the National Conference of Catholic Bishops to refrain from endorsing ERA as a group, although some have endorsed it as individuals. An endorsement from the bishops might have helped to undercut the religious arguments being used in Christian backlash circles to oppose equality for men and women, but it is questionable whether it would have much impact on Catholics themselves. A majority of Catholics (61 percent) already support the ERA according to a 1980 Louis Harris poll (compared to 54 percent of Protestants and 85 percent of Jews.) Furthermore, with a few exceptions—Illinois, Missouri, and Louisiana—Catholics do not account for significant numbers of citizens in the states that have not yet ratified ERA.

The opposition of privileged women to the ERA and to other issues raised in the name of justice by the women's movement underscores the fact that reality looks different to persons who view the world from a superior position than it does to those who view it from an inferior position. Women are divided.

Archbishop Raymond G. Hunthausen, leader of the Catholic Church in Seattle took note of this in October, 1980 when he issued a strong pastoral letter calling for justice for women:

> I am indeed aware that many, possibly a majority of women in the archdiocese do not view themselves as oppressed. This fact removes nothing of the pain of those whose study of social and religious history, and whose personal experience reveal inconsistencies in the religious doctrine of universal salvation when set against the realities of exclusion and discrimination. It is helpful to remember that one does not identify a present condition as painful or oppressive as long as there is no hope for improvement; we all protect ourselves psychologically from despair. It is thus imperative we continue to proclaim the message of hope, of the possibility for all peoples to advance as ever new persons toward the fullness of the Kingdom promised to all.

The Archbishop furthermore pointed out that "no one of us can achieve fullness as redeemed persons as long as anyone among us is the object of discrimination."

It is especially urgent that privileged women hear his words. Privileged women who insist on remaining on pedestals are likely to miss the injustices beneath them. They risk being among those startled folks at the gates of heaven who ask, "Lord, when did we see you hungry or thirsty or away from home or naked or ill or in prison and not attend you in your needs?" (Matthew 25: 44)

5

The Underside of the Pedestal

The trouble with the pedestal theory of women is that it is a myth for all but a tiny number of the women in the world. One woman's pedestal is supported by thousands of other women who are ineligible for pedestals.

We do not need to talk in faraway terms about ethereal, hoop-skirted ladies catered to by plantations full of mammies to care for their young and assorted other slaves to provide the economic support for the ladies' pedestals. We can talk about our own time and place.

For example, we run our society as if every family consisted of the ideal father earning a living, children happily eating cookies at home, and mother home all day to provide all the caretaking the family needs. In reality, only a minority of our families fit this picture. Yet the economic dependency implied for the woman in this idealized family continues to affect people in very different circumstances. A 1980 report from the U.S. Department of Labor concludes that *married-couple families with children under the age of 18 are far more likely to have two earners or more than were those families with no children.* Other facts which contradict the myths that justify women's dependency are these:

• Three out of five married couple families have at least two members working. Among such families that are black almost 60 percent of the wives are in the labor force; among whites the figure is 48.5 percent; among Hispanics, 46.3 percent.

• The assumption that married women work for "pin

money" is challenged by the fact that wives contribute an approximate 26 percent to family incomes. *Those who work full time contribute an average 40 percent.*

● A 1978 analysis of married women in the labor force showed that a third of them had husbands who earned less than $15,000. Ten percent had husbands earning under $7,000. These women were more likely to be working to buy oatmeal than to buy a second car.

● Although most working mothers are married, nearly one in four is divorced, separated, widowed, or has never been married. *Divorced mothers are more likely than any other mothers to be working or looking for work.* One out of every five mothers in the labor force is a single parent.

● One out of every seven families is headed by a woman. This is a startling fact. It reflects the rising divorce rate, and it has serious implications for our society.

● Families headed by single women (divorced, separated, or widowed, or never married) are more likely than any other families to be poor. In 1978, 42 percent of such families had incomes below the poverty level—compared with 15 percent of families headed by fathers only, and 6 percent of two-parent families. Over the last 20 years there has been a steady increase in the female-headed families that live in poverty while the number of other families living in poverty has been decreasing.

There are still a minority of families that can afford to choose a traditional family lifestyle in which the woman works exclusively at home. But to perpetuate the myth that this is an option for all families has some unpleasant and unjust consequences:

● Some people use it to rationalize the confinement of women to lower-paid, dead-end jobs in the labor force.

The Underside of the Pedestal

● It reinforces the assumption that housework is women's natural work. And so, when both partners in a marriage work outside the home, the usual result is that the woman has a second job: homemaker. It is not unusual for women to seek night-shift jobs in order to maintain a traditional family routine during the day. The only thing such women do *not* do, it seems, is sleep much.

What Happened to the Good Old Days?

It's popular among some people now to look with nostalgia to the Victorian era as a sort of golden age of family life when the traditional family functioned smoothly for the benefit of individuals and society. The pedestal theory of women was as prominent as the bustle in those days. The truth is different from nostalgia, though. In order to run one of those idealized Victorian households, it was necessary to have the labor of unpedestaled women who worked as servants. Without them it would have been impossible to maintain eight children and a home with as many bedrooms and still perch on a pedestal. Economics demanded that the wages of such domestic help be low, and in America a steady stream of immigrant girls provided a convenient base of support for upper-middle-class pedestals.

Just as some Americans are now profiting from the cheap labor costs in poor nations, a century ago privileged Americans profited from the poverty abroad which led millions to immigrate to America. These immigrants, the parents, grandparents or greatgrandparents of so many of us, did better themselves economically for the most part through the hard work in which they took pride. But we, their descendants, who have merely reaped the rewards of their sacrifices ought never to be so comfortable in our air-conditioned, four-bedroom homes that we forget the hard lives of those who made our own prosperity possible.

For those immigrants, there was no Social Security, no health insurance, no guarantee for widows and orphans. But there were long hours and miserable conditions in the mines, mills, stockyards, and sweatshops And the women immigrants were there along with the men, all ready hands for the new industrial economy. It is these people who ought to be on our minds when we drive past elegantly restored Victorian mansions that still line boulevards in American cities. For the working people of the Victorian era, it was no golden age of family life.

In addition, the Victorian myth of the happy domestic kingdom had another unsavory side effect. The virtuous ladies on pedestals embodied all the ideals of civilization, and, therefore, it was preferred that they be spiritual sorts, unblemished by lust and, in fact, incapable of enjoying sex. This was also useful for avoiding unwanted pregnancies. Therefore, when social critics and historians sift the dust under that fine Victorian lady's pedestal, they discover the sexual exploitation of women in the Victorian underclasses. Poor women, driven to prostitution, provided relief for Victorian husbands whose wives were not supposed to enjoy sex. Among the seamiest practices of the time was the business of providing proper Victorian English gentlemen with a certain delicacy their refined appetites sometimes craved—child virgins, some no more than 8 or 9 years old.

Though it is hard to match the hypocrisy of the Victorians, there is a sexual undergrowth on many respectable pedestals today as well. The privileged distance from suffering that social status and wealth confer on a few women sometimes also cloaks the fact that their husbands, pillars of the community, keep the prostitution business flourishing.

Wishing Does Not Make It So

When we look at the underside of the mythical pedestal and see the exploited class structure necessary to hold the pedestal in place, as well as see the sexual mold that grows on the pedestal's underside, we are beginning to see the situation of women as it is—instead of how people wish it were. And yet no matter how much evidence accumulates to contradict old wishful thinking, some people only grow more insistent that the wished-for situation is the way things really ought to be. And they insist more loudly than ever that God also wishes things to be their way.

When the frosting of religion is spread over injustice, the results are particularly distasteful, especially for people who value both religion and justice highly. How, such people ask, can people claim to care about mercy or justice and continue to ignore the reality of women's lives? How can they dismiss the evidence that women's economic and psychological dependence often results in cruel circumstances for women? And, above all, how can they ignore the ways in which religion itself encourages—and in some cases *demands*—the dependence of women on men?

Our religious values have long reinforced a separate system of economics for women. The women's system of economics is based on belief that women will get married or pregnant and leave the labor force. Therefore, employment practices which treat all women as temporary workers—excluding them from training programs, confining them to

80

low-paying jobs, requiring them to resign when pregnant— are permissible. Lower wages for women are justified under such a system, because women's wages are presumed to be "supplementary"—needed perhaps for luxuries but not for basic support for a family.

A new member of the personnel department of a small U.S. electronics company ran into this attitude when she tried to eliminate sex stereotyping from company hiring decisions. As the first woman to hold anything but a clerical job in the personnel department, she was eager to put her feminist beliefs about equality into practice. Now she says, "I was naive to think I could make much of a difference all by myself."

The workforce of the company was mostly women who made between $3 and $5 an hour performing monotonous tasks involved in the assembly of electronic components, using microscopes and tweezers for much of their work. The ideal employee, the company management believed, was a married woman whose children were in school and who wanted to work for "pin money" or "extras" such as television sets or vacations. There were no males on these tedious assembly lines.

"The first time I had to hire assembly-line workers," the new personnel interviewer recalls, "unemployment was high and I was deluged with calls, including a few from high-school boys. The male foremen were not happy when I sent some of those boys to them for interviews, but eventually a few boys were actually hired for the assembly lines. One foreman, though, was more stubborn than the rest. He continued to reject every male applicant I sent him, and finally one day he came into my office to complain. 'Stop sending me boys to interview,' he said. 'Their hands are too big—and besides the work is too boring for them.' For some reason he didn't think the work was too boring for women."

Such hiring practices frequently result in keeping production costs down because some managers believe the threat of union organizing is less in an all-female workforce. And, or course, this attitude flourishes in countries providing cheap female labor for industries that then provide bargains for American consumers. Our economy continues to benefit from sexism in other countries as well as in our own.

We even confront boldfaced economic sexism under the guise of religion. In March 1979, *Christian Century* magazine reported the story of John F. MacArthur, Jr., pastor of Grace Community Church in Sun Valley, California, who told his congregation that wives and mothers should not work outside the home. In keeping with his principles, the church fired several of its secretaries.

"If you can't live on what your husband makes," MacArthur said, "then you're living beyond your God-intended means." The pastor and an all-male board of elders furthermore agreed that unmarried women, including those widowed or divorced, with children, must depend on relatives or the church for financial support.

It is hard to understand how people who say they live by teachings of love and justice can turn away from the results of women's dependence on men, especially when women are faced with divorce or the death of a spouse.

While the women's movement is not concerned only with economics, it is very important to realize that woman's economic dependence on man narrows the choices of her life and can make her psychologically dependent on him for her very identity as a human being. In Western countries a woman usually signs away her name when she marries, becoming her husband with a "Mrs." in front of the name, signifying that she is an extension of him now.

Supposedly by marrying, the two have become one, but in reality he is increased, and she is decreased. She is asked again and again at parties and on registration forms to identify her social status and income by answering the question "What does your husband do?" (Yet she prefers this question to having to answer the other familiar question: "What do *you* do?") Years of this sort of thing erode a woman's self-confidence. She comes to feel that who she is, what she has, where she is, and even *why* she is all depend on her husband.

The consequences to women of being so dependent upon men become painfully apparent when their spouses die or divorce them. And when this happens, those churches that support a system of sex discrimination share the responsibility for the injustices that confront the woman, for the reality of her life when she can no longer count on her husband's goodwill.

The Meek May Inherit the Earth—But Not the Farm

When marriage ends, a woman's economic vulnerability is painfully clear to her.

When Lewis Nordby, a Minnesota farmer, died in 1976 his wife Leona had to fight to keep the farm that they had purchased together in 1948 out of joint savings for $12,000. Over the years they had operated the farm together, borrowed money together, and maintained joint bank accounts.

The farm was held under joint tenancy, and the Minnesota law requires the surviving joint tenant to pay inheritance tax on the entire joint asset unless the survivor can prove a contribution in "money or money's worth." Leona

Nordby, despite years of farm work, could prove no such contribution, because all income taxes had been filed in her husband's name only. She faced the prospect of paying inheritance taxes on a farm which had appreciated in value to $176,586.

Leona Nordby was successful in obtaining a tax-court ruling that during her marriage there was an "implied agreement to share profits," and she avoided inheritance taxes. Nevertheless her case and similar cases in other states point out how vulnerable widows can be when there are substantial assets such as a farm or family business at stake. Since tax returns and legal documents are often in a husband's name only, widows sometimes have difficult times proving their contribution to the joint assets. Widows—and not widowers—have this problem, because the widow's contribution to joint ventures is often a nonmonetary contribution, and that is sometimes difficult to prove.

While the Nordby decision is an encouraging one for some widows, it still contains problem elements. It does not make clear whether a nonmonetary contribution to an asset would include housework. And a ruling by the state attorney general's office excluded housework as such a contribution. The law remains unchanged; the survivor of a joint tenancy property must prove a contribution in order to avoid inheritance taxes on the entire asset.

When marriage ends because of divorce, the pain of economic vulnerability can easily be compounded by the sex discrimination that, for the first time, a woman acknowledges seriously. Not only is she often at the mercy of her husband financially, but she is also the victim of sexist attitudes held by lawyers and judges.

Marilyn is a woman who learned about all these things

the hard way. A few years ago other women might have envied her for her spacious home and neighborhood of high-income professional and business people. The neighborhood seemed almost too good to be true. And it was. Today, at the age of 55, just beginning to gray a little, Marilyn looks around at the other lovely houses nearby where other middle-aged women like herself are starting over, too. There are enough women in the same boat now for a bridge group, but none of them have time for that sort of thing these days. They are working or going to college or both. The men who used to live in the houses with them are gone now. They are starting over, too—with new, younger wives.

"It's just so unfair," Marilyn says angrily. "I see so much talent and such intelligence in these women. It's just so unfair that a man can effect that kind of destruction in an individual who has helped him become what he is." But there is little new in the divorce stories of this neighborhood—women who followed the usual pattern of merging their dreams with a man's dreams, working to help him achieve those dreams with the expectation of sharing in the rewards someday. Their share is over now.

Marilyn was stopped cold at her first divorce hearing when it became clear to her that the law did not recognize her share in the marriage. When she and Tom had married 18 years ago, Marilyn was already 37 years old, and she had a good job as an executive secretary. She brought to the marriage 35 acres of land that she had bought and paid for herself as an investment for her future. That land served as collateral for all the property the couple later accumulated under Marilyn's shrewd management. Through Marilyn's contacts, she arranged 100 percent financing for large investment properties, including their house and rental property. She did virtually everything to manage the property, including cleaning the rental property when necessary. At the divorce hearing, management of the property was awarded to Tom.

All Marilyn received from Tom was child support for two years until their son, an only child, turned 18. This, despite the fact that Tom owns his own business and has an annual income of almost $100,000. Because Marilyn has worked throughout their marriage, she will be able to support herself—in contrast to many other women who in mid-life find themselves divorced and unemployable. Marilyn is in one way lucky: Her income is $28,000. But this fact has worked to her disadvantage. She is convinced the male judge and the male lawyers (her own included) have the attitude that on such a salary Marilyn can take care of herself quite well and will need little more. "That's a good salary *for a woman,*" the young attorney Marilyn hired to represent her told her.

The point all these men are missing is that Marilyn wants a just settlement that reflects her contribution to the marriage—including her 18 years of working double duty as an executive secretary and as a homemaker providing Tom with the freedom and security to start his own business. Her work freed him completely to concentrate on his own ambitions. During that period Marilyn and Tom were also paying alimony and child support to Tom's first wife and children.

"The hurtful part of it is that he can walk away from it without any responsibility," Marilyn says in the weary monotone of an exhausted woman.

"My husband *expected* me to work when we got married even after I had a child. He *expected* me to play the traditional role, making bread and doing all the things around the house—even painting the house. And he *expected* me to take care of his things. So during the lifetime of our marriage, I became a do-it-all kind of person. I brought in a very good salary. I worked a full day. Took care of his dogs. Entertained lavishly on the holidays. Only once in a while did I have a cleaning person. He also had a large garden, and I was *expected* to can and freeze everything that came out of there—at the same time as helping to produce it in the garden. He had continuing dreams of starting a new business, and each year he added one more thing to my list of chores."

Sadly, Marilyn looks out the window at a beautiful, tree-shaded lawn. They never had a vacation in 18 years of marriage, but now that they are separated, Tom is planning a $2,000 trip to Florida. It hurts.

"The only time he spent with us really was through his gardening. And through his dogs and through his showing off all of his *things*. I did all the accounting and all the tax preparations. I took care of his animals, including taking them to the vet whenever they got hurt."

In effect, Marilyn—like so many women—was living Tom's life, not her own. She wonders now how it happened to her. She had been an independent woman when she married him.

"Then I changed my whole self around. I thought I was keeping my independence, but I was wrong."

Marilyn grew up believing "the man's the boss." She never questioned it. From childhood she saw herself as a willing and hard worker for others. Why? She has just begun to ask herself that.

"I started working for other people so young that I thought that was the way to survive."

But if Marilyn ever assumed that those she took care of

would in turn take care of her, she knows now she was wrong. When her divorce is final, she will have no health insurance nor pension. Several years ago Marilyn had wanted to start a pension plan for herself. Tom discouraged it, because he had already set up a generous pension plan for himself, which would be more than enough for the two of them to retire comfortably. Besides, Marilyn's investment properties were meant to provide additional retirement security. As for health insurance, Tom told her his company's health insurance was a better policy than hers, and so she dropped her own. Moreover, the company Marilyn works for may soon go out of business. Worried about her future now, Marilyn asked her employer's attorney to set up a retirement plan for her. After all, she pointed out, she had been with him for 20 years. "You've gotten a good salary all these years, and that really takes care of it," the attorney told her.

Wherever she turns these days, Marilyn feels she is being judged in a system with two sets of rules—one set for men and one set for women.

"Even my own attorney, a young man, when I explained my job to him—what I do and why a man would be paid $40,000 a year to do the work I do—his comment was that I should be glad I was able to work!"

Marilyn now feels the best divorce settlement she can even hope for is a split on the property. "That just depends on how effective his attorney is. That's the only hope. I can't get anything out of his pension. The referee in the first hearing made it very clear to me that he doesn't have to provide any medical or hospital insurance for me either."

One word missing from the vocabulary of all the men involved in Marilyn and Tom's divorce is equality. "I feel my attorney now wants me to get out of it," Marilyn's voice rises out of control for the first time and she chokes, *"what a woman should."* She is silent for several long seconds. "The divorce decree tells you what the rest of your life is going to be. I'm not getting what I deserve—justice."

Those Merry Widows and Gay Divorcees

Ironically, Marilyn and other separated and divorced women think the women's movement may have backfired for them. Judges assumed that they were able to earn their own way and so they required less from their ex-husbands. But others believe that judges have *never* given women fair divorce settlements, and myths about generous settlements are dispelled by the facts:

● One in 20 women receive alimony. There are no reliable statistics available on how many men default on such payments.

● Only about 60 percent of divorced women with children at home had an award or an agreement for child support in 1978, but Census Bureau statistics show that half these women received less than they were due. The average annual child support payment was $1,800, and the average total income of women receiving child support was $8,940.

● Women get no credit in divorce settlements for the years they spend at home being homemakers.

As one expert on domestic law observes, "Society speaks to women out of both sides of its mouth." Homemaking careers are praised, but women may be penalized for choosing them.

There is a whole new class in America these days. They are middle-aged, downwardly mobile divorced women, women such as Marilyn, who are examining the assumptions on which their lives are based:

● "I divorced, had three children to raise alone, and discovered my total earning power was, at top, $800 per month," said one such woman. "My former husband was earning around $30,000 annually, but the courts said I had a profession—teaching—and thus they did nothing about housing or enforcing child support. The fact that there were no teaching jobs did not seem to enter into the picture; the men behind the benches seemed to think I was lying."

• An executive vice president of a Fortune 500 company forbade his wife to resume her career as an executive secretary, saying he was "not going to have any wife of mine pound a typewriter." That was a number of years before he divorced her.

When he divorced his wife, the man's attorney successfully argued that monthly alimony payments should be terminated after four years since the woman had once held a well-paid secretarial position and could be expected to again obtain a job that would pay her between $12,000 and $18,000 a year.

The court ignored the fact that the woman had not worked outside the home for 23 years. She was 45 years old.

The husband, who was 46, at the time of the divorce was earning well in excess of $120,000 a year.

Life, indeed, isn't fair.

There is considerable lip service paid to the value of homemakers, but few people, except for those who are or have been homemakers themselves, really understand the intelligence, skill, and organizational ability needed to do the job well. Nor do they understand how much a homemaker contributes to the family.

"The private sector thinks housework is trivial: having homemaker on a resume is about as helpful for getting a job as listing 'ex-convict' or 'long-term mental patient,' " concludes a report by the Minnesota Council for the Economic Status of Women.

Ms. magazine printed the following "Help Wanted" notice—tongue in cheek, of course:

> HELP WANTED
>
> REQUIREMENTS: Intelligence, good health, energy, patience, sociability. Skills: at least 12 different occupations. HOURS: 99.6 per week. SALARY: None. HOLIDAYS: None (will be required to remain on stand-by 24 hours a day, 7 days a week). OPPORTUNITIES FOR ADVANCEMENT: None (limited transferability of skills acquired on the job). JOB SECURITY: None (trend is toward more layoffs, particularly as employee approaches middle age. Severance pay will depend on the discretion of the employer). FRINGE BENEFITS: Food, clothing, and shelter generally provided, but any additional bonuses will depend on financial standing and good nature of the employer.

Divorce almost always reduces a homemaker's standard of living, frequently to poverty.

Returning to the labor market does not mean equality, especially when a woman's absence from the labor market has been spent making social contacts and entertaining to enhance a man's career. "The day after my divorce," said Jeanne, an intelligent and attractive woman who had been helpmeet and hostess for a rising corporation executive, "my husband went back to his $50,000-a-year job, and I went back to my $600-a-month job. We were never again equal after that day." Her $300-a-month child-support payments do not rise with inflation.

U.S. Census Bureau figures show the median income of

women who worked full-time all year in 1977 was $8,620 compared with $14,630 for men in the same category—59 cents for every dollar men earned.

Although 43 percent of the U.S. workforce consists of women, sexism combined with women's life patterns (which are strongly determined by sexism and sex-role conditioning early in life) result in a disparity between men's and women's earning power. Women who drop out of the labor market during child-raising years do not have the seniority or experience that often result in higher incomes. Women have also tended to choose work—or have been guided by school counselors and parents to choose work— in lower-paying fields. They chose clerical work instead of higher-paid sales work or business management; nursing over medical school; working for others over starting their own businesses. More than a third of employed women work in clerical jobs. Only 5 percent are in middle management, and less than one percent are in top management.

In 1979, the median income for families maintained by women was $220 a week, compared to $350 median income for families maintained by men. And families maintained by women alone are almost three times more likely to have incomes below the poverty level than families maintained by men alone; seven times more likely than families in which there are two parents.

The Social Security system is less than it promises for economically vulnerable women. A widowed homemaker under the age of 60 who does not have children under 18 at home is ineligible to collect Social Security benefits from her husband's account unless she is totally disabled. Usually, unless she has adequate pension benefits and excellent insurance, such a widow must look for a job. At this point in a woman's life she learns not only about sexism but also about ageism.

There is a bitterness as well as hardship in the stories women tell about their financial situations as they move toward what they had thought would be retirement. One 58-year-old woman spent her life raising five children while her husband, a railroad engineer, was on the road. He was among the minority of employees not covered by Social Security, since he was covered by the Railroad Retirement Act—an act which provides no benefits for divorced spouses. After 36 years of marriage, the husband divorced his wife, and she became ineligible for any retirement benefits from any source whatsoever. Not only were her chances of employment limited by her age and by her lack of work experience outside the home, but she suffered from failing eyesight and arthritis.

Even when an ex-husband is covered by Social Security, a divorced homemaker cannot collect benefits from his account unless the marriage lasted ten years. This, however, is an improvement over the previous requirement that the marriage had to have endured for 20 years before a woman could collect benefits.

Even though Social Security was meant to be sex neutral, the system's benefit structure is not equal for men and women because of the possibility of divorce and because women are frequently absent from the labor force during their working years.

The system also has another inequity that, in effect, penalizes some wives who are *not* totally dependent on their husbands. Consider the Andersons and the Browns:

The Andersons are an employed husband and a wife who has always been a homemaker. For Social Security purposes, Mr. Anderson's lifetime earnings averaged $1,000 a month. In retirement their monthly benefits are $648—his benefit of $432 and her "spouse benefit" of $216.

The Browns also averaged lifetime earnings of $1,000 a month when their joint earnings ($667 for him and $333 for her) were combined. But their monthly retirement benefits total only $544—$325 for him and $219 for her. Since the "spouse benefit" is half of the wage earner's benefit, Mrs. Brown's retirement spouse benefits would have been $162.50, not much less than the benefit she earned for herself, considering that she and her husband paid double social security taxes during their working years.

Knocked Off the Pedestal

In addition to the other injustices that accrue to women as a result of the sexist structure on which their lives are based and as a result of the cruel sexist myth of the pedestal, there is an aspect of injustice that is not class conscious. It affects not only those women never eligible for pedestals anyway, but also those idealized women on pedestals themselves. Privileged women are as eligible for it as prostitutes are. This injustice has no respect for doctoral degrees or Anne Klein suits.

It is called by various things: wife battering, wife abuse, domestic violence. It has various manifestations: beatings, rape, psychological torture.

But all manifestations of this problem have one thing in common: They knock a woman off her pedestal unmistakably and ought to be enough to disabuse the most piously romantic woman of the notion that she can really live her life securely on a platform above other people.

Wife abuse is widespread, and it is a problem that crosses race and class lines. Even suburban zoning restrictions don't help. A poll by the Gallup organization revealed that fully one American in five is personally aware of one or more serious cases of child and/or spouse abuse. One estimate is that half the wives in this country have been beaten at least once, but no one really knows what the true extent of wife abuse is. Most families are inclined to keep such painful embarrassments secret.

Again, sadly, religious values often enter the picture, woven as they are into the imperfect fabric of lives that rip apart in violence.

The very idea that some men believe they have the authority to abuse their wives is frequently an outgrowth of twisted religious principles: "I was brought up to be a good wife and serve my husband, and I've done that," the woman in her 40s told a counselor at the shelter for battered women. She finally had come to the shelter after years of being beaten by her husband, an alcoholic. On other occasions the woman had gone to her priest for help. His advice to her was always to go home to her husband and try to get in him into treatment for his alcoholism. But the priest said nothing to affirm her own belief that she had a right not to be beaten. In fact, the shelter at which the woman finally found protection was publicly opposed by some members of the clergy when it was first opened. They charged that it would promote feminist ideas that would result in the break-up of families!

Religion also affects violent families because of the religious value that the family must be preserved at all costs. "Till death do us part" has sometimes meant death to women. While individuals clearly must sacrifice for the good of the family, such sacrifice should not have to include enduring abuse.

A Christian counselor of battered women believes that the Christian image of "suffering servant"—suffering for others—has adversely affected wives who find themselves in a situation of being beaten by their husbands.

Again and again women report that they have gone to their clergymen for help in such situations only to be told to "offer it up" or "try to forgive him." The emphasis is on saving the marriage rather than protecting the life and limb of the woman being abused.

Irving Greenberg, a professor of Jewish studies at the City University of New York and director of the National Jewish Resource Center, draws an important lesson from Jewish history that relates to wife abuse. The lesson is about power and powerlessness. And the lesson is especially important for those women who reject the idea that men ought to share power equally with women.

During the Holocaust there were some Jews who collaborated with those in power, their Nazi persecutors. They thought that by so cooperating they would escape the fate of those Jews being sent to the gas chambers. Their powerlessness was corrupting for them and for their powerful oppressors.

Powerlessness is not compatible with human relationships, Greenberg explains. Good will is irrelevant. Potential victims should have the power to protect themselves, and "no one," he says, "should be dependent for her existence or security on the goodwill of others."

Nevertheless too many women have not learned this lesson about the ways in which powerlessness corrupts them.

They continue to perpetuate the corruption of relations between men and women, joining in the call for wives to be submissive to husbands. The Total Woman movement and similar courses of instruction for women sponsored by Christian churches are means by which the powerless participate in the backlash against women searching for a basis of justice in their relationships with men.

The powerlessness of battered wives includes the fact that often they have nowhere to go and no means of support aside from their husbands. They are totally dependent on the men who are beating them. Even if they obtain welfare payments to help them establish separate residences, such women may be unable to find a landlord who will rent to a woman with children. And even then, court orders do not necessarily stop a violent husband from breaking into a wife's apartment and beating her yet again.

A nun who directs the social-justice work of a rural Catholic diocese describes the widespread and largely hidden problem of wife-beating in the mostly rural area of church-going people in which she lives. People live in isolation there. The problems that arise in families are dealt with in a framework of rugged individualism, independence, and secrecy. She often receives anonymous calls from women who have been beaten by their husbands and wonder what to do. In rural areas there are rarely emergency shelters available to such women. Even in cities where there are such shelters, the experience has been that they cannot begin to accommodate the numbers of women who need help. In a rural setting, the church may be the only place an abused woman can turn for help.

Certainly religion was a factor in one farm woman's desolate existence. In fact, her husband would not allow her to leave the farm except to attend church on Sunday—and that was with him. The man had much to hide. He beat his wife regularly. He refused to let her leave the farm to shop. Five of their nine children had not received their routine immunization shots. Usually the beatings arose from his anger at her frequent pregnancies. Yet the man refused to consider using any form of birth control, including abstinence. Ironically, when she became pregnant with her tenth child, the husband beat her and tried to get her to agree to an abortion. Finally the woman contacted the county sheriff, and it was the sheriff who brought her and the children at last to a shelter for battered women.

Because of the role that religion does play in wife abuse, it's appropriate for religious people to take leadership in helping the victims of abuse and in the prevention of abuse. In some conservative Christian communities, however, instead of support for shelters for battered women and family violence prevention programs, there is suspicion that such things interfere with the family and further "government interference" in private lives. Senator Paul Laxalt's so-called Family Protection Act has similar restrictive provisions relating to spousal abuse and child abuse: "No Federal program, guideline, agency, action, commission action, directive, or grant shall be construed to abrogate, alter, broaden, or supersede existing state statutory law relating . . ." to such abuse. People who value the lives and health of women and children must ask *who* is protected from *what* with such a law.

Instead of forming a wagon ring around families, wouldn't it be more of a Christian response to help heal the victims of family violence and to attempt to change those responsible for it?

The great founder of the Catholic Worker Movement, Dorothy Day, once told some of her followers that every local parish ought to have a safe house of hospitality for people in need. Catholic Workers in Minneapolis run one such place. In the first four years of their shelter it provided safety for more than 500 women and 300 children.

Another Christian response to wife abuse is to challenge the traditional sex role stereotyping that leads some men to think they must dominate their wives and even, in the worst extremes, *own* their wives as property.

"The man who beats up his wife, you can counsel the hell out of him, but send him back into a context in which he's expected to be the boss, and he's going to hit her again," said one professor who conducted national research on family violence. Such research shows that households in which husband and wife share decision making are the least violent households.

"Go do something for the men," one woman told an archbishop who wanted to visit her shelter for battered women to show support for the work she was doing. "Go get the men and let them live in the rectories!" Why, she wondered, should it always be the women and children who have to leave the violent home? The churches, in her opinion, would be doing something valuable to counter family violence by working against the legitimization of both violence and sexism.

One member of the clergy who is doing just that is Rev. Marie Fortune, a United Church of Christ minister who runs the Center for the Prevention of Sexual and Domestic Violence in Seattle.

Fortune believes that if our society is serious about saving the family, we must deal with family violence, a problem that is literally destroying families. And she believes that the clergy have an important role to play in the treatment of family violence, since questions often arise about the nature of marriage, family, divorce, and suffering during the counseling of the victims of family violence.

"The most common response we receive from clergy (pastors, priests, rabbis) when we try to involve them in training or educational events about sexual or domestic violence is: 'But no one ever comes to me with these problems,'" Fortune reports. "We quickly point out that the reason that 'no one' comes to them is probably *not* because no one in their congregation is experiencing these problems.

"What we have is a classic vicious cycle: people experiencing sexual or domestic violence hesitate to go to their clergy out of fear, embarrassment, shame; clergy continue to carry the mistaken belief that 'no one in my congregation has this problem.' It is not necessarily that there is a lack of concern on the part of clergy; rather it is a lack of awareness and priority.

"At the end of a four-week clergy seminar on sexual and domestic violence, one of the pastors said that he didn't know what was happening in his parish but that he had had two incest cases and a rape in the past four weeks. We discussed this with him and discovered that the first Sunday after he had begun the seminar, he had announced from the pulpit that he was receiving this training and expected to find it helpful. By saying this, he communicated: 'I am aware, concerned, and available to deal with the problems of sexual and domestic violence.' And people began to seek him out for help."

But most of the clergy are not prepared to deal with these kinds of family problems, Fortune believes:

"Our national survey of parish clergy indicated that congregants do go to their clergy with personal problems—just not problems of rape, child sexual abuse, and spouse battering. Unless one understands these problems and how to identify them, a clergyperson will seldom ever 'see' them."

The "Protection" Racket

Has women's fear of physical abuse been used to manipulate women into compliance with tradition? Do men offer women protection for good behavior—protection, that is, from themselves as well as from other men? It's interesting to think about such questions.

A girl who hitchhikes or who walks alone after dark without a male escort is generally thought to be asking for trouble. If she is attacked, some people are inclined to blame her as much as her attacker.

Women learn to assert their independence with caution.

Sexual harassment is a nasty little by-product of sexism that women have always lived with, but now, thanks to the women's movement more and more women are getting the courage—and, more important, the legal power—to fight it. One young black woman successfully sued her employer for not acting promptly to stop the sexual harassment to which she was subjected by three male employees on repeated occasions. For months the young woman endured humiliating insults, including a reported remark by one man that he wished the days of slavery would return so that he could train her sexually and turn her into "his bitch." One man repeatedly patted her on the buttocks, and, another one of the men grabbed her between the legs as she bent over a machine. When she complained to her supervisor, he told her to expect that sort of thing working with men. There was nothing, he said, that he could do about it.

Even in bright daylight on a crowded city street a woman alone is not safe from psychological attack. The catcall, the whistle seem so harmless to most people. Women even sometimes joke that the wolf whistle by a young male stranger is a crude compliment of sorts: "I'll worry when they *stop* whistling at me," one woman confides to another in a tone that suggests both exasperation and amusement at unfathomable male ways.

But the catcall, the wolf whistle, the "Hey, what's your hurry, Baby?" remarks on city street corners are not harmless compliments. They are an insidious form of psychological abuse that seeps into the pores of women. For what these casual street corner encounters say to a woman is this: "Watch out, woman. Step out of line, and I'll get you. You may think you're some sort of princess, but underneath you're just another woman. You're all the same."

And if this seems to overstate the case, watch how often women receive wolf whistles when walking down the street with male escorts. A man is protection. From other men.

If you are with a man, it is a signal that you are someone else's property—or that you might be someone else's property—so you are *not* fair game. The street male has something to fear himself by accosting you. At a young age, a girl learns that a man is protection.

Independence in women triggers resentment in some males. And as a new genre of movies shows, it sometimes triggers more than resentment. As the women's movement gained wide acceptance among Americans, horror movies began to appear showing women as the victims of gruesome torture, murder, and rape. This in itself was not new. What was new is that the women victims were *independent* women, and the films enlisted the sympathy of the audience on the side of the *attackers,* not the victims. Instances were reported in which men in movie theaters actually applauded the attackers. Apparently, these movies touched something special in the psyches of some American men. To women the message in these movies is the same as the streetcorner catcall: "Step out of line, and I'll get you."

Of course, resentment against independent women manifests itself in more subtle and acceptable ways. Pornography, while not subtle, is at least quiet. Then there is the not-quite-pornography magazine that college-educated men "only buy for their excellent articles." In recent years the women featured in the magazines (in the photos, not in the articles) have included a number of allegedly liberated women. Most questionable of these were the nude girls of the Ivy League colleges.

It is impossible not to wonder about the young women who actually posed for such pictures. But the motives of the male editors seem wonderfully transparent. It is as if by displaying such photos of supposedly independent women, the magazine is able to make a statement that amounts to roughly this: "You think, Woman, that you are liberated and different from other women? This ought to show you that underneath your blazers and your advanced degrees you are still the same—just another woman."

6

Women Against Themselves

It's true. Women *can* be their own worst enemies.

If the things men believe about women are distortions of the truth, they are nothing compared to the lies women believe about themselves. The institution of sexism is so ancient, so ingrained in human behavior, that women have often supported it as whole-heartedly as men. They have regarded it as the natural order of things, the way things are.

Even at the end of the 20th century there are many women angrily fighting the efforts of feminists to tell the truth about women's lives. "Those feminists are witches . . . they are just miserable women . . . dissatisfied with their lives and they just want us all to be miserable, too," a Stop-ERA member tells a reporter. There is a deep division between this woman and other women today. But then women have almost always been divided.

And that is our greatest weakness.

Eve's Bum Rap

Many women see themselves through the eyes of men. They use men as mirrors to look at themselves. And something very basic inside of them does not like what they see. In order for women to support sexism in this way, or perhaps, *because* they support it, these women actually dislike— even hate—themselves.

Along with this, they may dislike and distrust other women as well.

This is not surprising really. After all, as little girls women are taught that a member of their sex was responsible for sin in the human race. Later they are told that *they* are responsible if a boy becomes sexually aroused, and, therefore, the responsibility for whatever happens lies with the girl, not with the boy. And there has never been any question that when "whatever happens" the consequences belong to the girl, not the boy.

No wonder that the current wave of feminism had barely begun when t-shirts began to announce: "Eve Was Framed."

This initial distortion of religion, however, has become a giant lie over the centuries. Women have internalized it by accepting their second-class status as God's plan.

And what are the results? Repressed anger. Guilt. And an epidemic of depression.

Religious Perversion

They did not like themselves, those women. Those women who throughout the centuries were ashamed of their menstruation. "The curse," they called it, instead of welcoming it as a creative force that marked them as a vital part of nature.

Women were taught not to touch their bodies, not to find pleasure in them. In some places their genitals were mutilated—the sort of thing that still goes on with little girls in Africa today.

It is hard to imagine how such distortions could have taken place without the cooperation of women themselves, and it is intriguing to wonder whether women's lives would actually have been different if Jesus' attitude toward women had prevailed past the first century.

But it did not. Instead women adopted religious symbols of their inferiority into the new religion.

> Any man who prays or prophesies with his head covered brings shame upon his head. Similarly, any woman who prays or prophesies with her head uncovered brings shame upon her head. It is as if she had had her head shaved. Indeed if a woman will not wear a veil, she ought to cut off her hair. If it is shameful for a woman to have her hair cut off or her head shaved, it is clear that she ought to wear a veil. A man on the other hand, ought not to cover his head, because he is the image of God and the reflection of his glory. Woman, in turn, is the reflection of man's glory. Man was not made from woman but woman from man. Neither was man created for woman but woman for man. For this reason a woman ought to have a sign of submission on her head. . . ." (1 Corinthians 11: 4-10)

In his next sentence, Paul balanced this passage somewhat with an acknowledgment that women's bodies are indispensable to human life:

> Yet in the Lord, woman is not independent of man nor man independent of woman. In the same way that woman was made from man, so man is born of woman; and all is from God. (1 Corinthians 11: 11-12)

How tragic for women and men that the miracle of birth through women's bodies, a process which confirms men's utter dependence on women, was not celebrated as such. Instead women consciously and unconsciously regarded their genitals—and often themselves—in derogatory terms they learned from men.

It is easy to criticize other women for having ceded their bodies to men and having tried to escape from their bodies in various ways. But we cannot forget what a source of pain those bodies were to them. They were raped. They suffered uncontrollable pregnancies, miscarriages, births. They endured abortions. They hemorrhaged. For some women their bodies really were nothing but trouble.

So there is really cause to celebrate now as women are reclaiming their bodies. Thanks to the women's movement, the back-to-nature ecology movement, and mostly to a generation of sensible young mothers, women have rediscovered the beautiful power within themselves.

An increasing number of women have discovered that they can regulate their fertility without the use of chemicals by simply learning to understand the natural rhythm of their bodies better.

Birth itself is no longer an occasion for the operating room unless there is a reason to expect complications. Some women are opting to give birth at home or in specially planned, home-like rooms in clinics. There has long been a movement to return to natural childbirth without drugs or other means of diminishing a mother's role in the birth process. And fathers, the forgotten people of childbirth, are increasingly helping with births—an experience which many find exhilarating. Breastfeeding, too, has been reclaimed by young mothers, though earlier generations were told it was old-fashioned.

(An unhappy added note to this, however, is that the baby formula manufacturers who promote bottle feeding have been seeking out new markets in extremely poor countries such as Haiti and Columbia where new mothers are told that bottle-feeding is the modern way. Without safe drinking water with which to prepare formula, diarrhea and malnutrition often result, and many babies have died. The practices American women are discarding are now being urged upon poor women of struggling nations.)

Barriers Among Women

The alienation of women from their bodies was helped along because women were also alienated from one another. This happened—and still does happen—with the aid of physical barriers among women such as convent walls, veils, and illiteracy. But more important, it happens because of the *roles* assigned to women and women's own difficulty in reaching one another across the barriers created by these roles. Even the most intimate woman roles, mother and daughter, can be barriers for women who long to reach the person inside the role.

Moreover women are often resentful of other women who step out of prescribed feminine roles. Envy is a powerfully destructive emotion among women. And equally destructive are the ways in which women try to avoid being envied by other women—not dressing or behaving differently from the group, not excelling outside of feminine spheres, and so on. "Inertia and envy are sisters," says Madonna Kolbenschlag. As she sees it, the powerful backlash against the women's movement is "an overwhelming expression of envy":

> It contains the recognizable features . . . fear of another's success, self-pity, blind trust in past security, identification with a clearly defined subordinate social role. As with subcultures and

primitive peoples, it is a reactionary response to anyone capable of creating change. (*Kiss Sleeping Beauty Good-Bye,* 1978)

Even in the New Testament we have an example of woman's resentfulness when another woman steps out of the expected role.

"Lord, are you not concerned that my sister has left me to do the household tasks all alone? Tell her to help me." Martha was clearly upset with her sister Mary. Mary had seated herself at Jesus' feet to listen to him when he came to visit them. Martha was feeling sorry for herself, left alone to prepare food for their guest. Who did that Mary think *she* was anyway!

"Martha, Martha," Jesus replied to her, "you are anxious and upset about many things; one thing only is required. Mary has chosen the better portion and she shall not be deprived of it." (Luke 10: 40-42)

There are still Christian women who have a difficult time with that passage of Scripture. They identify with Martha, for they have been in her shoes many a time. They struggle with a voice inside them that says, "Why should I be here in the kitchen doing all the work and *she's* out there enjoying herself?"

This resentment spills over into other circumstances, too. It flourishes in neighborhoods where a woman and her children are set apart with the words "their mother works." It is alive in the women who choose careers as homemakers and community volunteers for themselves but make disparaging remarks about other women in the community who do not choose the same careers—or who cannot afford to choose the same careers. Since in many neighborhoods now women who used to be available as volunteers for schools and churches are now employed during the day, those who are still available to volunteer end up with even more requests for their time. Often they feel like resentful Marthas left to do Mary's share of the work in addition to their own.

Throughout the history of the church, women have been carefully separated from one another. This was easier to notice in the days when all nuns wore habits. So many of those habits were distorting garments that quite effectively concealed the fact that a living, breathing woman with an actual body was inside the habit. Nuns were supposed to be better than, well, just women. And so in the 1960s when nuns began to wear ordinary street clothes, it disturbed a lot of people to discover that nuns were women after all.

The habit is a symbol that nuns were to be set apart from other women. They were elite, living in protected convents, receiving education beyond what laywomen might expect to receive, often performing work of professional, missionary, or mystic nature. With their veils they were "brides of Christ," not to be touched by other men and—providing they behaved themselves—worthy of special respect and privileges in the church. Though, of course, they were not on the level of male clergy. And male clergy wrote the rules governing the nuns.

Offering independent women the option of becoming nuns was a way for the church to set them apart from other women. Other women were destined to marry, a vocation that was distinctly inferior to a religious calling. Becoming a nun meant increased status for a woman. She could transcend her carnal womanly nature and become more like a man. No wonder there are those who still have difficulty accepting nuns in street clothes.

A woman who would be so independent as to reject both marriage and the convent was in the past a discomforting phenomenon in the church. She was expected at the very least to *act* like a nun and *hope* to become a wife. Some communities of Christians still do not quite know what to do with the single woman. She is a shadow person in the church, writes Joan Ohanneson: "In a sense the church has neither the time, the money, nor the energy for singles. Its agenda centers on marriage and family; any deviations from this pattern cannot help but constitute a nuisance institutionally." (*Woman: Survivor in the Church,* 1980)

The confinement of women to specific roles within the church resulted in alienation of nuns from laywomen. Laywomen found it difficult to see beyond the habit and discover a genuine woman like themselves. And nuns found it difficult to see behind the laywoman's roles of wife and mother. Restricted to their separate roles, they focused on their differences instead of on their common womanhood.

The rigid distinctions between nun and laywoman began to blur, however, when nuns began to modernize their clothes and lifestyles, socializing and working more and more with lay people. At the same time, lay people began to assume increased responsibility in local churches, the result of the Second Vatican Council.

Yet there are people who are very uncomfortable that distinctions are being blurred. It upsets a sense of order, a hierarchy of roles within the church. And this is why some nuns, some of whom head large U.S. religious orders, currently believe there is pressure building to restrict the new freedoms of nuns, including the trend among nuns to dress in a way that does *not* distinguish them from other women.

In the church and in society, women have also been divided by barriers of class and race, by privileges and by poverty. Even though reform-minded women of privilege have devoted a great deal of time and money to their attempts to improve the lives of poor women, the barriers among women remained fixed in place.

There were examples of the barriers among women during the early struggles for women's rights in this country, just as there are now. Few working-class women were attracted to the woman's suffrage movement in the beginning. To those worn-out women who worked in sweatshops and mills for ten to 12 hours a day and were paid almost half of what men were paid, the issue of voting rights seemed remote. "For them, equality also meant better pay for their labor, security from fire and machine hazards or the unwanted attentions of a foreman, and a chance to get home to their domestic tasks before complete exhaustion had overtaken them," writes historian Eleanor Flexner.

Flexner also tells us that women, *privileged women,* were among the barriers to women's achieving the vote until 53 years from the time of the first state suffrage referendum:

> Almost without exception the women in [the antisuffrage organizations] were ladies of means and social position. The main burden of their argument was that woman suffrage placed an additional and unbearable burden on women, whose place was in the home; the fact that this argument came largely from women whose housework was done by an adequate force of servants and that they presumed to speak for women less fortunately placed, never seemed to disturb the "antis," who also argued that they did not need political suffrage since their menfolk represented them and cared for their interests.

Among the other interests involved in keeping the vote from women were the liquor interests. They helped fund the movement opposing woman suffrage, fearing that women voters would do their business interests no good. If women obtained the vote, their sympathies were unlikely to be with brewers and distillers. Of course, as we have already noted, the antisuffrage movement had the endorsement of the Catholic hierarchy and the eloquence of their Irish-American tongues and pens.

There are parallels to this today with much of the opposition to ERA coming from privileged women whose cause is advanced and subsidized by conservative men claiming to have women's interests at heart.

Yet today there are people who believe that the women's movement is responsible for creating a barrier among women, too. This is ironic, since the thrust of the entire movement is to overcome the barriers among women. But the women's movement is blamed for downgrading the role of homemaker, for "putting down housewives." True or not, that's what many people think.

Sociologist Jessie Bernard urges her sister feminists to think about how they may have contributed to a division between themselves and the homemakers who are suspicious of feminists:

"To what extent, if any, has the feminist position about the drudgery of housework also been an expression of class attitudes, of an elitist disdain for manual labor and a commitment to careers as the one route to success? Are we working so hard to improve the economic and legal status of homemakers that we forget their social status, that having to play up the negative of their economic and legal status in order to support new legislation to overcome them have the unintended effect of denigrating the homemaking position as a whole?"

Women who are full-time homemakers do often chafe these days at the question they encounter wherever they turn: "What do you do?" Some of them do blame on feminists the lack of confidence they hear in their own voices when they reply, "I'm just a housewife."

Their feeling is not universal among homemakers, though. Many homemakers are feminists themselves. They look to the women's movement as a vehicle by which to fight the sexism that puts them in a vulnerable position economically and legally because they choose to perform a valuable role for their families.

But it is counter-productive to spend much time arguing whether it's the sexist system or the feminists that put homemakers down. Women who expect equality with men must, of course, extend it to one another—and get on with it.

Unfortunately women have had more experience working against one another than working together. A college professor, writing about what she called "the frigid sisterhood" among women academic colleagues, describes a system in which "the message beamed by those in power to women at every level" is "to succeed, separate yourself from other women."

Dolores Frese, of Chicago, learned some hard lessons about such barriers among women when she was an assistant professor of English at the University of Notre Dame. In the end, she became a principal plaintiff in a class-action law suit, which spearheaded the first really united effort of women at the university on their own behalf. Yet when she first began teaching at Notre Dame, Frese said that she, too, discounted the stories of discrimination told by other women:

"When I first came, there were some women who were on their way out, and they were extremely angry and disgruntled and radicalized and vocal. I didn't pay as much attention to them as I should have. I was on good terms with them, and I kind of heard with one ear the things they were saying. It's the old story of what has happened to women again and again. I believed that there must be some secret fault in their case that I didn't want to pry into. I didn't want to conduct an investigation. I didn't want to think ill of them, but I was sure that there was something that I didn't know about that made them unacceptable, because the university clearly wanted to have women. I mean, they had hired *me*, hadn't they?"

But a few years later, Dr. Frese would charge the university with sex discrimination for denying her tenure and furthermore accuse the university of a pattern of such discrimination by maintaining a revolving door of lower-paid women faculty members who were denied tenure so that they could be replaced by a fresh group of lower-paid faculty members.

"For this reason, when people say to me, 'Doesn't it make you angry that the women on campus have not come forward and surrounded you with support?' I say, 'No, I understand every single one of them. I understand. I was that way myself for my first two or three years here until I got batted down.' I thought some of the things that had happened sounded strange to me, but I was willing to listen stereophonically. The good things that were being said in one ear muffled the bad things that were being said in the other ear."

Women Against Themselves

Dolores Frese and other women at Notre Dame and elsewhere who have taken similar risks have learned that it can be a lonely experience to confront sexism and demand to be treated justly. It is loneliest when those against them include other women.

7

Women Together

If the barriers that separate women from one another prevent women from seeing the truth of our common lives—and our common lies—then the first step for women seems obvious: We need to remove those barriers that separate us—nun from laywoman, black from white, feminist from nonfeminist, lady from whore. We are all women.

This is what the women's movement is about, women coming together, learning that together we give one another strength to accomplish what we had despaired of doing individually.

Of course, there is nothing new about the mere act of women gathering. Women gathering together to cook, to work, to gossip, to wash, to harvest—these are ancient rituals. With the women's movement, however, women began to come together in a different way. We still shared experiences, but now we share the *truth* about our experiences as well.

Overcoming Barriers

One of the hardest truths to face is that women themselves can be barriers for other women. Never socialized to prize teamwork with other women and used to identifying with an individual man for status and life direction, it is sometimes harder to convince women themselves of the need for equality between the sexes than it is to convince men.

So it is crucial that women start overturning the barriers

that separate them. The isolation in which so many women live their lives—isolated, that is, from other women who share their experience—is a veil that clouds their vision and keeps them separated by such things as social class, race, religion. If women are to achieve justice for themselves and for other women, they must overcome temptations to regard one another as competitors or even as opponents merely because of a difference in point of view.

Is it mere wishful thinking or naivete to suggest that women find ways to focus on the things that unite them instead of the barriers that divide them? That they put aside the thinking that divides them as either feminists or nonfeminists, nun or laywoman, believer or nonbeliever, black woman or white woman, professional woman or secretary?

Women have spent centuries brooding about the things that divide them—or unfortunately, when faced with personal achievement, rejoicing like the Pharisee about their own superiority to others of their sex. Our separateness is an obvious source of our weakness, despite our numbers. Just as obviously, we will overcome our weakness by overcoming our separateness.

Setting aside all that divides them, women must attempt to focus instead on all that unites them. They have recently allowed the family to become a hostage political issue, but the fact is that there are family issues that elicit concern from a broad spectrum of women: Concern for women's health, in pregnancy and childbirth, in menopause and old age; concern about the high incidence of depression among women; concern about wife abuse and child abuse; pornography and child pornography; nutrition, environmental, and peace issues; decent affordable housing for the elderly (most of whom are women) and for poor families with children (many of which are likely to be headed by women). While women can always hide safely behind the barriers that divide them, goodwill and openness (or honesty) will provide many more avenues by which they can come together and work in common for justice—justice due other women as well as themselves.

The Women's Movement

At its best, this is what is going on with the women's movement in the United States today. Even though its critics like to portray the women's movement as a group of radicals or elitists bent on destroying the family, the movement is really an amalgamation of women from many backgrounds and classes and races. It is most powerful in its ability to reach across all the established barriers and create a common consciousness in which a middle-aged woman who has seldom been outside her New York Jewish ghetto shares many of the same beliefs and sense of urgency as a young black woman in Oakland or an Irish Catholic graduate of Rosary College.

That is the women's movement at its best. But it seems wise to admit here that the women's movement, like the church or democracy or anything else touched by human hands, is not always at its best. The women's movement is not at its best when it contributes to divisiveness among women with a paranoia that permits no disagreement and labels any criticism as the work of the enemy. If there is polarization among women, the women's movement has contributed to it just as the opponents of women's equality have contributed to it. In this, feminism might as well admit its mistakes just as it asks others to admit theirs. The point is not to dwell on past mistakes but to move beyond them.

That, too, is the point of feminist efforts to call attention to injustice for women: not a reverse witch-hunt but a demand to set things right.

Nevertheless the achievements of the women's movement have been many and their effect on American society sweeping. Beginning with consciousness-raising groups in the 1960s and early 1970s, women began to come together, shedding their isolation, and sharing their anger, doubts, and problems. They set in motion a process, still unfinished, of identifying why they were considered inferior to men and how they could change this false ideology of male superiority.

Free from powerless isolation, feminists substituted the opposite belief that there was power in numbers. Sisterhood became the ideal, "Sisterhood Is Powerful" the slogan.

Early advocates of woman suffrage in the 19th century were not much interested in organization. Susan B. Anthony appeared on the scene later and made her greatest contribution to the cause of women's rights—her devoted, disciplined, and tireless organizing ability. She knew that speeches and writing helped, but victory belonged to those who knew how to count—and knew how to organize to get the count they needed. The cause of women's rights was her entire life. In her first petition drive for the cause, she introduced an innovation that is now a standard political method—enlisting 60 women as captains, one for each county in New York State. Together they braved primitive travel, hostile receptions, and lack of money to collect 6,000 signatures in ten weeks.

There were to be many more hardships and campaigns for those early advocates of women's rights. It would be 66 years from the time of that first petition drive of Susan B.

Anthony until women's right to vote was secure in the constitution, and Susan herself would not live to see it. *One of the lessons history teaches us, though, is that the cause of women's rights did not advance until women united, organized, and fought to secure their rights.*

When the current wave of feminism began in the 1960s during an already politically charged era, women needed no further demonstration of the necessity for organization. The National Organization for Women (NOW) and many other feminist groups were founded and soon became a political force.

Women forged coalitions to influence legislation, organized class-action law suits to fight sex discrimination in employment, banded together to help rape victims and express their outrage about pornography and sexual harassment, and started cooperatives and collectives around such issues as health care. When a government report was issued saying the Pill carried negligible risks for women, the Women's Health Network was there to object and to present documentation that the government report was biased, because a drug company that stood to profit from sale of the Pill had financed the study that led to the report. Women had begun to take responsibility for the decisions that affected their lives.

But many people watched in dismay as some feminists' insistence on controlling their own lives became equated with an adamant position in favor of legalized abortion. The "pro-choice" people demanded with deep conviction that a woman be free to choose whether or not to bear a child. They did not accept what others believed with equally deep conviction—that the fetus is fully human from the moment of conception, and, therefore, abortion is murder.

121

The more that this position became equated with main-line feminists, the more some Christians became convinced that it was not possible to be both Christian and feminist. Just as women had started to overcome their old barriers, the abortion issue became a new barrier between them.

Feminists of Faith

If there are people within Christianity who believe that Christianity and feminism are mutually exclusive terms, there are feminists who feel the same way. But it is wrong to say that all feminists reject religion. Some do, of course. Others are very much a part of the Methodist Church or the Catholic Church or the Presbyterian Church. They are Quakers and Unitarians and many other denominations, too. Still others are experimenting with new ways of knowing God divorced from patriarchal religion.

What all feminists do have in common is a recognition of the sexist structures of religion. But feminists hold widely different views on what to do about it.

One extreme is a radical woman-centered religion. Having experienced intense feelings of alienation in mainline churches, with their male leadership, male images of God, and, some believe, male morality, women who gravitate toward woman-centered religious experiences are seeking female images of God and religion in which women share power with one another. They want none of the trappings of hierarchical authority they associate with mainline churches.

Yet others believe reform is possible without women having to separate themselves so. They see themselves as loving critics who want to help heal the sin of sexism within religion. Their effort is to integrate their feminist principles and religious principles.

Writing in the evangelical Christian magazine, *Sojourner,* Joyce Hollyday makes a distinction between secular feminism and her own understanding of Christian feminism:

> There is much that we can benefit from in the secular feminist movement. Our Christian faith, however, will temper many feminist expressions of power. We cannot view the world as if it holds a limited amount of power, of which we are entitled a portion. This view will only create competition among oppressed groups.
>
> For us, power means taking control of our own lives so that we can give them away. We must continue to look to Jesus as our example. Jesus' power was immersed in servanthood; his life was one of submission.

Both feminism and faith come in so many variations that it is difficult to generalize about them except to say that under both banners there is room for many kinds of people. Feminists of faith do provide something of a bridge between alienated women and the sexist religious structures from which they are alienated—the churches and the synagogues that have blessed women's repression throughout history and called it God's will.

And to the women's movement, feminists of faith contribute a needed dimension. Feminism needs a soul as well as a body lest it end up with the same distortions that the Church Fathers achieved by embracing Greek dualism of body and soul. Just as the Women's Health Network is dedicated to helping women reclaim control of their bodies, feminists of faith are dedicated to helping women regain control of their own spirituality. By doing this, they are contributing to a wholeness for women. Women are learning to love their bodies and their spirits as one, their whole selves. This is healing work.

Feminists of faith challenge their sisters in both camps: those feminists who have not yet decided where they stand on the question of faith and those believers who do not want to acknowledge the religious justice implicit in much that goes by the name of feminism.

A New York feminist, raised in the Jewish faith, had set aside her religion for years, but when she and her husband applied to adopt a baby she was faced again with the question of faith. At first, she said, "it was just a terribly pragmatic thing" because the adoption application form required adoptive parents in her state to specify what religion they would give their adopted child. Believing their chances for getting a baby could increase or decrease depending on what religion they specified (since the birth mother could indicate a preference for the religion in which she wanted her baby raised), the potential adoptive parents were in a quandary.

"Then," the woman related, "I had a dream that was just overwhelming. It was my father, and he was furious at me for abandoning my religion." She couldn't shake the questions generated by the dream. Not even after a private adoption was arranged and completed without the couple having to indicate in what religion, if any, they would raise their baby girl.

"Since then, I felt that I should really think about this," the new mother said. What would her daughter be missing if they did not belong to a synagogue and attend regularly? Does she want such a traditional choice? Or is there an alternative? Something perhaps more in harmony with her feminist principles? She really does not know yet what her answer will be. What she does know is that she must have some sort of answer before long.

But as faith is a challenge for feminism, feminism is a strong challenge to communities of faith. This is especially true considering the sexism incorporated in those communities.

Feminist consciousness cannot be said to have ignited any blazing prairie fires among the grassroots of religion yet. But here and there questions of justice with roots in the women's movement are surfacing:

- Why can't girls be altar servers?
- Why should the pastor's wife be expected to share her husband's work at no pay?
- Why aren't more women in decision-making positions in the church?

One question, however, cuts through all the other questions to the heart of male supremacy: Why can't women be priests?

Women's Ordination

Although women can hardly be said to have avoided discrimination or obtained prominent leadership in Lutheran, Presbyterian, Methodist, and other denominations, they at least are not excluded from the ministry on the basis of sex.

In the early 1970s, the question of ordaining women took on new meaning when it faced the Episcopal Church at a time when it seemed that feminism was toppling one sacred cow after another. In 1974, three Episcopal bishops ordained 11 women illicitly, and the controversy about women priests reached a higher pitch until at last, in 1976, the general convention of the Episcopal Church voted to permit the ordination of women.

The Episcopal decision gave new hope and new energy to the budding movement for the ordination of women priests within the Roman Catholic Church, whose liturgical tradition was similar to the Episcopal Church tradition, but whose pyramid-style authoritarian government was vastly different from the democratic structure of the Episcopalians.

Although it is not widely known, a woman had petitioned the Vatican for ordination to the priesthood in 1962 during the Second Vatican Council. Dr. Gertrud Heinzelmann, a Swiss lawyer and woman suffrage leader, was alone when she petitioned and alone when she was rejected by the Vatican.

Thirteen years later in the United States women began standing together—and men began standing side by side with them—with the goal of opening the priesthood of the Catholic Church to women. Buoyed by U.S. feminism and the promise of reform in the church following the Vatican Council, 1200 people met in Detroit in 1975 for the first conference on women's ordination in the Catholic Church. Several hundred women there said they believed they were called to the priesthood.

Who were these women, and where did they get such ideas? Extraordinary as their goals seemed, the women themselves turned out to be ordinary women in many other ways. They were a mixture of ages, of laywomen and nuns, of single women and married women. Some of them worked as hospital chaplains. They counseled people, helped them resolve their problems and make peace with God. When they had reached this point with a person, they wanted to be able to bless that moment somehow. It seemed to them artificial and wrong to bring a person to that point only to have to fetch a male priest to, in effect, finish the job. Some of the women had wanted to be priests since childhood— just as Jeannette Piccard, one of the first Episcopal priests, had wanted to be a priest from the age of 11.

The official response of the Roman Church to the women's ordination movement in the U.S. church came in 1977 in the form of a declaration. Women, it said, could not be priests, because Jesus was a man and only men could represent him. (Earlier a commission of church biblical scholars had reported there was no conclusive evidence one way or another in Scripture regarding the issue of ordaining women.) Tradition, however, was overwhelming.

Far from silencing U.S. advocates of ordination for women, however, the Vatican declaration fanned the flames of the controversy and helped open the eyes of many women in the Catholic Church. Some women who had been until then only mildly interested in the issue of women's ordination were outraged at the suggestion that men could present an image of Christ and women could not. The Vatican declaration against women priests actually boosted the women's movement within the church.

A second women's ordination conference was held in Baltimore in 1978. Most of the 2,000 people there were women from the U.S., but there were also representatives from Latin America, Europe, and Africa to address international interests, for the women there recognized that the church had international interests. It was not merely an extension of white, middle-class America in which middle-class women could simply extend American notions of equality.

There was much discussion in Baltimore as to whether

127

the women who feel called to the priesthood really should be seeking entry to a system that other women believe is basically corrupt, based as it is on a patriarchal power structure. Some women thought ordination for women was important merely as a symbol; what was really needed by the church was an abolition of the entire clerical power structure to enable the church to get back to being the sort of community that the original followers of Jesus had in mind. But other women wanted only to serve people, and they saw ordination as a way to do this more fully. Many of them already had earned Master of Divinity degrees, and for all practical purposes they were already doing priestly work.

From the perspective of the Baltimore conference the issue of ordination for women in the Catholic Church seemed complex. And yet the issue remained essentially simple: a matter of justice.

If women cannot be ordained, then there must be a reason. So far no reason has been advanced that does not connect the church to a sinful history of sexism. And sexism aged for almost 2,000 years and relabeled "tradition" is still sexism. And it is wrong.

Ordination for women is an issue that cuts through many other issues to the core of sexism. It is a broad challenge to our thinking. Through it, we are beginning to learn how we have made God a victim of sexism, too.

Although we say that God is neither male nor female, our language tells us otherwise. Now we are learning to think of God in feminine images as well as masculine ones. God our Mother, God our Father. For some people this is unnerving. For others it seems insignificant ("How can you get worked up about sexist language when people are starving to death in Africa, etc.").

But language is not insignificant. It reflects what we see and believe is real. Increasingly, women feel excluded when they listen to sermons that tell them all *men* are *brothers* (rather than all people are brothers and sisters or neighbors) or sing songs about the faith of their *fathers* (especially when they recall that it was their *mothers* who often kept the faith). Their objections to noninclusive language that may have once been acceptable but no longer is acceptable should be heard. Gradually they are being heard. Acceptance of some language changes by U.S. Catholic bishops was a step in this direction. More remains to be done.

Women Ministering to One Another

Women are not rejecting their spirituality; they are reclaiming it. What they are rejecting is the idea that a man—whether husband, priest, or gynecologist—is an essential intermediary between themselves and God's creative, healing power. Increasingly now, women are realizing the importance of ministering to one another.

It is hard to imagine any woman ministry that attempts to overcome more barriers to bring women together than the Institute for Women Today. It began as an idea of Sister Margaret Ellen Traxler, a Catholic nun, and Anna Wolf, of the American Jewish Committee on Women. Initially, this ecumenical effort aimed at reaching middle-class women in churches and synagogues to increase understanding of the religious and historical roots of women's liberation. Now the institute, with an office in Chicago, is also the means by which some privileged professional women are able to be connected with some of the most underprivileged and oppressed women in our society, women in prison.

The institute enlists the services of more than 20 "faculty" members who help provide service at the Cook County Jail in Chicago and several women's prisons. They teach prisoners poetry, creative writing, journal writing, and drama. A full-time women's advocate at Cook County Jail accompanies inmates to court and helps them solve personal and family problems. Weekend in Prison sessions provide teams of lawyers and psychologists for consultation by women prisoners.

Margaret Traxler explains that the prison program grew out of her visit to Jane Kennedy, a Chicago nurse who served a prison sentence for burning draft records during the Vietnam War. "Our women need role models," Jane Kennedy told her. "We need to see women who have made the grade, who have succeeded."

One of the first members of the institute's prison faculty was Dorothy Day, social activist and founder of the Catholic Worker Movement. "Only Dorothy Day, with her long history of serving the poor, could respond to the question of an elderly woman at Alderson (federal prison in West Virginia)," Traxler remembers.

"Why are you here?" the woman asked.

"We have come to wash your feet," replied Dorothy Day.

There are many other ways in which women are ministering to one another now, too. It may be a group of feminists who organize a shelter for battered women in their town. Or a group of women engaged in prostitution and trying to change their lives, meeting together to find support and self-esteem. Even in traditional parish churches, it is not unusual to find women ministering to one another in prayer groups or organizations for the divorced and separated.

And there is an "underground" movement of women

alienated from mainline religions. Finding themselves unable to participate anymore in regular worship services that are conducted only by men and use noninclusive language, these women meet together and form their own communities. In these communities they are seeking a new style of shared decision making that could someday be a model for renewed communities of men and women.

But whether they do it in religious settings or outside religious structures, whether they do it formally or informally, women are ministering to one another now. They are overcoming barriers that once seemed formidable. Together they are finding strength to do things that never seemed possible before when they were alone.

Should Women Leave the Church or Reform It?

There is no denying that many Christian women are now engaged in a process of recognizing the sin of sexism within the church as well as in society. They are expressing anger that they have long repressed and identifying the pains within them that they dared not identify in the past.

Many women have already left the church because of sexism. They have given up any hope they ever had of achieving justice for women through the church, because they believe that sexism has become essential to the functioning of the Christian church. Many more women could end up taking this step to leave the institutional church in the future unless they can somehow hold on to their hope that the church really is moving toward equality of men and women.

There are still many women who find the arguments for staying with the church are more compelling than the arguments for leaving it. They believe reform is possible, and quite a few of them believe that their own mission in the church is to make this reform happen.

During the Vietnam era, many supporters of the U.S. government's policies glued to their automobile bumpers a defiant bumper sticker that told antiwar or disenchanted citizens: "America: Love It or Leave It." Many Christian feminists have decided to love the church, not leave it even though the church at this time in history falls far short of granting women the full personhood they believe is rightly theirs.

But loving the church, as Christian feminists see it, means telling the church the truth—whether the church wants to hear it or not. "To speak the truth in love" is how Theresa Kane has defined the mission of Christian feminists in the church today.

By no means do Christian feminists deny the good that exists in the world today because of organized religion, nor do they deny that as individuals they have experienced good and liberating moments through the church and through other persons of the church. But because they love the church, they insist that the church must do a better job of living up to its own message. The church cannot be a witness to justice in the world when the church itself is mired in injustice. Christian feminists believe that their own mission in the church is to call the church to acknowledge its sin of sexism and repent.

"There does not exist among you Jew or Greek, slave or freeman, male or female. All are one in Christ Jesus." Christian feminists believe that this ideal is still possible. However, some of them believe that this ideal will be possible only when the church eliminates its hierarchical, patriarchal structure that requires for its survival the suppression of women—the idea, that is, that there is a hierarchy among human beings that is part of a divinely-created order, and that in this hierarchy some men hold the power over other men, and all men hold power over women.

"If there is no longer a need to suppress the Spirit who moves Christian women to fully participate in theology and the church, then Christian theology and community can become fully liberated and liberating," writes Elisabeth Schussler Fiorenza. "Church Fathers and theologians who do not respect this Spirit of liberty and freedom deny the Christian community its full catholicity and wholeness. Feminist theologians and Christian feminists will obey this call of the Spirit, be it within or outside established church structures. They do it because of their vision of a Christian and human community where all oppression and sin is overcome by the grace and love of God."

8

Men Apart

As women experience second thoughts about the traditional roles they have lived and experiment with new options for themselves, the lives of men are changed.

Men have responded in various ways to the women's movement. Ridicule. Disbelief. Suggestions that all "uppity feminist" women needed was a good man. And then, when men realized the logical implications of what the women's movement was saying (and there were some men who realized this before their wives did) some of them reacted with anger, deep-rooted anger. Perhaps, some of them subconsciously realized their inability to hold back an idea whose time had come at last. Such men provided excellent targets for women's own anger.

The anger women experienced was a long-suppressed anger at having been socialized into auxiliary human beings, passive assistant persons, part of a sex whose unchallenged function was to support and further the human existence of the *principal* sex, men. These women found it logical to direct their anger at men. Indeed, it was frequently a bitter, screaming rage. And so, people who wanted to discredit the ideas advanced by the women's movement found one more reason to do so: They dismissed all feminists as hysterical man-haters.

But most women do not hate men. The explanation for women's status is too complicated to place the blame exclusively on husbands or fathers.

Men As Spectators—Cheers and Jeers

Men find themselves apart from women in women's struggles with their roles, with their powerlessness, with their anger. That men were and are apart is nothing extraordinary, though. They have been socialized to be apart from women through different experiences when they were boys ("You don't want to be a sissy, do you?"), through football teams and all the institutions that set men apart. Whether in the priesthood, at Harvard, or on the golf course, men have been apart from women. And women have been apart from men. So it was only natural that men and women had different perspectives on reality when the canyon separating them began flooding with the ideas and questions that surge through the white water energy of the women's movement.

Men were apart, and men still are apart. But they are not the enemy. They are, most of them, spectators, spectators watching with confusion and frustration and sometimes with sympathy and understanding, with jeers and cheers.

There are many men who want their college-aged daughters to have equal opportunity and fair access to medical school; yet they want their wives of 25 years at home, and they want the house clean and dinner on the table when they themselves arrive. But as inconsistent as they are, these men are changing, just as the women around them are changing. As spectators, many men have been supportive of women, the individual women in their lives and women in general.

Women who want to avoid the arduous road to equality by hating men and blaming men would do well to consider the results of the poll released in 1980 by Louis Harris showing that support for the ERA is stronger among men

135

than among women, whose rights it is designed to assure. Men backed the amendment 59 percent with 35 percent opposing it. Women backed it by 54 percent, with 38 percent opposing it.

The Canon Law Society of America, an organization of mostly Catholic priests, studied and endorsed ERA as did individual Catholic bishops, while the largest organization of Catholic women in the country refused to do likewise.

Other evidence suggests that some men are quicker than some women in realizing that the issues raised by the women's movement are matters of simple justice. A study of a cross section of American Catholics commissioned by the Leadership Conference of Women Religious and conducted by the Gallup poll organization found that 32 percent of American Catholic men interviewed favored opening all positions in the church, including the priesthood, to women gradually or immediately. Of these men, 41 percent cited justice as the reason. Women responded differently to the survey. Only 28 percent of those interviewed believed that all positions in the church should be open to women immediately or gradually. Of these, only 29 percent believed that the expanded role for women in the church was a matter of justice. More often women interviewed felt that the role of women should be expanded because women had special abilities to contribute to the church.

One shudders to think that this result might be interpreted to mean that women know themselves best, and if they themselves believe that there is no injustice in their status, they ought to have the weight of the argument on their side.

It seems more likely that women, who have suppressed the truth about their lives for so long in order to merely survive, do not always find it a simple matter to face the truth. It is painful to say to oneself, "I have been wrong all these years. My life and the lives of all women are built on an inequality that violates truth and justice. I have lived a lie. I must change no matter how much it hurts to tell the truth and demand justice." It is easier by far to say, "As a woman I am especially well qualified in certain human activities, expecially those emotional areas in which women have always been superior. I have so much to offer that society can only be enhanced by permitting me to offer it." The woman who says *only* this continues to deny the truth that her life is based on inequality.

Can it be that men, who have not had to invent such lies about themselves to survive an inferior status, can be more objective about recognizing injustice when they see it? We should note, though, that men have had to live with long-established lies that have justified their superior status and the patriarchal system that has institutionalized numerous privileges for males. But there is a difference in a lie that sustains a person in a privileged position and a lie that bandages an open wound. Both are equally wrong and equally corrupting, but the latter sort demands frequent changing and firmer application to stop the flow of blood.

Honest and sensitive men have recognized the lies in their own lives as well as those in women's lives. Some have even taken great risks to themselves in order to bring their lives in line with the truth. It was a great risk, for instance, for three bishops of the Episcopal Church to ordain, publicly and with full ceremony, women as priests before their church convention had authorized such a step. Of course, the women who were ordained were equally courageous, since they were consigning themselves to public condemnation and rejection. But the point is there *were* men willing to take risks along with women in the name of justice.

Other men, intelligent, even champions of justice under certain circumstances, have been sensitive enough to begin questioning the status quo, if not following it to logical conclusions. John Quincy Adams, former president of the United States who ended his career in old age as a congressman from Massachusetts, in 1838 was among the first to defend the rights of women from the floor of the House of Representatives. His words seem harmless enough today, but at that time they were in sharp conflict with the prevailing beliefs, beliefs which stubbornly persist in some places even today:

"Why does it follow that women are fitted for nothing but the cares of domestic life, for bearing children and cooking the food of a family, devoting all their time to the domestic circle—to promoting the immediate personal comfort of their husbands, brothers, and sons? . . . The mere departure of women from the duties of the domestic circle, far from being a reproach to her, is a virtue of the highest order, when it is done from purity of motive, by appropriate means, and the purpose good."

As spectators in women's struggle, men have not been entirely insensitive or uncaring or even unhelpful. But they have all remained apart. Because of this, they can be sympathetic, but they do not know what the experience of woman is.

The late John Howard Griffin, a white man, darkened the color of his skin so that he could travel through the South as a black man. In his book *Black Like Me,* widely read in the early 1960s, Griffin described the changes he underwent as he began to fear and experience life in this new way. Something along this line would be needed for a man to experience life as women have experienced it.

One psychotherapist who tried an experiment with this in mind found that men had a more difficult time exchanging places with women than the other way around. She asked men and women to close their eyes and imagine themselves to be members of the opposite sex. Women reported feeling more powerful: "I was King Kong, and it was great," one of them said. But men reported difficulty in visualizing themselves as women.

"I didn't *want* to visualize it," one of them said truthfully.

Most men cannot conceive of themselves as females. While it is common for little girls to wish they were boys, and while "tomboys" are affectionately tolerated, the opposites are not true for little boys. They certainly are not encouraged to wish they were girls, nor are they usually permitted to engage in the "effeminate" behavior of playing with dolls. While it is not unusual for a bright woman to be "complimented" with a remark that she "thinks like a man," it is an insult for a grown man to be told he "thinks like a woman." Boys get the message early: girls are inferior. Girls get the message, too.

The *History of Woman Suffrage* records one instance when men did learn what it felt like to be women. It was at the third woman's rights convention ever held in the U.S. On this occasion, which took place in Salem, Ohio, no men were allowed to speak:

> Never did men so suffer. They implored just to say one word; but no; the President was inflexible—no man should be heard. If one meekly arose to make a suggestion, he was at once ruled out of order. For the first time in the world's history men

learned how it felt to sit in silence when questions in which they were interested were under discussion.

But not all men are willing to be sympathetic or even just neutral spectators. Some of them are neither perplexed nor frustrated. They are positively hostile to women's struggle for equality. Such men provide an easy focus for women's anger because they so willingly and so neatly fit the model of male oppressor and enemy. Often such a man has a view of the world that cannot afford to admit equality for women. Were he to do that, his entire world would crumble.

Such a man may be the most charming fellow in town. He may be the best provider on the block. He may be the sterling husband who never forgets to send his wife a dozen red roses on her birthday; the proud father who displays his children's portraits on his office wall. But his benevolence and his success rest upon his requirement for a certain kind of order.

His is a world divinely ordered and unchanging. It is a world that relies on authority. It is a world of "father knows best" and "wait 'til your dad comes home." It is an orderly, predictable world in which he is the head of the family and his wife is the "heart;" in which he does the hard-headed thinking and she provides the emotional climate that softens their existence. He does his part; she does hers. He provides the paycheck; she makes sure the shopping and cooking get done. When they disagree, order demands that she submit to him. Their reward for right-thinking and hard work is, if not really bliss, a peaceful order.

When such a man looks around him and sees rampant disorder, he knows exactly where to point a finger. Are their friends divorcing? Is there a drug plague at the local junior high school? Is the country soft on communism? Well, it is all part of the chaos that results from the disorder of the women's movement—as he sees it, anyway. In his eyes, when women began to neglect their duties to their families, the whole order began to crumble. He began to lose control. His privilege, his authority began to erode. Even if he succeeded in keeping the women's movement away from his own wife and family, such a man could not help but perceive a threat in what he saw going on in numerous other families around him. Or he might see it in his company's affirmative action policy, which now makes it necessary for him to compete with women for promotions as well as with men.

Blame for disorder is on women who disrupted the world as he knew it, a world which seems to him to have worked well. It certainly worked well for him. His breakfasts were prepared for him, and he came and went with unquestioned freedom; he had stature, comfort, and a clear script written for him telling what was expected of him for the rest of his life.

The idea that women's quest for equality is somehow responsible for the disorder in the universe is a perverse notion, but a notion that is nevertheless consistent with the idea that Eve is responsible for the eviction of the human race from the Garden of Eden. The interpretation of the biblical story of Adam and Eve has caused trouble for women throughout Judeo-Christian history. The uncritical acceptance of the idea that man fell from a state of grace through women does nothing to substantiate man's claim to superior decision-making ability that makes it the natural order for him to have authority over woman. And the equally absurd notion that women's equality will upset the

141

delicate balance of nature is but a desperate and inevitably doomed attempt to reassert a singular form of male-minded order that amounts merely to male dominance.

We can get a sense that some of this disorder may have been precipitated by very early attempts at truth telling and justice in the early Christian communities. Those who today pray for and argue for a return to what they call Bible-based order are avid readers of the New Testament letters in which St. Paul instructs early Christians about the proper roles of women.

Too Much to Lose

Among the men who stand apart from women is another group that would regard the overtly oppressive men we have been discussing here as rather crude intellectually. In contrast, these men tend to fancy themselves as sophisticated, even intellectuals. They see the logic of women's equality. They see the justice of many of women's demands. They may even function as coaches or cheerleaders for wives or friends trying to work out strategies for career goals. They may be influential mentors for ambitious young women at the office. Yet in the end, these men opt to stand with their cruder fellows who are more open about their wish for a universe ordered in their image and likeness. In the end, the faint-hearted intellectuals are sympathetic to women's wishes to be equal human beings, but they cannot afford to follow their sympathy to its logical conclusions.

Theirs is a deliberate selfishness. They see in women's equality a diminished stature for themselves. If there are to be no more merely "token women" in the office or the department or the shop, that means that women will begin to compete with men in territory previously restricted to males. Since men will no longer have the advantage, their own odds for success will be narrowed.

It is one thing for such a man to encourage his wife to resume her career after their child is born; it is quite another for him to restrict his own career, limiting his travel and overtime to permit him to assume half of the child care. Or there is the man who does not want children and insists that his wife take a health risk with the Pill or have an abortion for his own convenience. These men deceive themselves about their openness to equality for women. They have too much to lose.

Men as Victims

Besides being spectators to women's struggle for equality, men are also victims of the same sexism that grinds women down.

It is difficult for women, who have waited on men and soothed their egos, to see men as victims. They have seen men occupying only the privileged place, commanding more pay, wielding all the power. But men have lived a lie just as women have lived it, and so in the sense that those who live in untruth are the victims of that evil, men as well as women are victims of an unjust order.

Men are victims because the demands of malehood place limits on their ability to express the fullness of human emotions. The fact that men are more likely to have heart attacks than women illustrates how stressful the demands of malehood can be for its victims.

The military draft is another area in which men obviously are victims. Only young men are expected to die for their country. Women are beginning to conclude that this is a particularly awkward form of discrimination. On the one hand, women do not want their daughters to die anymore than they want their sons to die, and yet they realize that when a nation drafts only its young men it is doing several things:

- It is discriminating against young men by placing the entire risk of being killed or maimed on them;

- It is exempting young women from such danger and telling them, in effect, that they are privileged to escape such responsibility;

- It is, on the other hand, undermining any claims women make to equality with men, since they do not bear equal responsibility.

How, women are asking, can they claim selective equality? If a woman's place is not in the ranks of the army how can she claim a right to equal representation in the ranks of the federal bureaucracy or IBM? Once we start asking where is a woman's place, we are back where we started—with two separate places, one for men, one for women.

Women's nonparticipation in the military has cost them. Veterans' preference is a system meant to give returning veterans priority in civil service job openings. Although it seems a decent way for a nation to show its gratitude and respect for the men who served in the armed forces, it is nevertheless a system which has worked against women's advancement.

The U.S. Commission on Civil Rights in 1978 referred to veterans' preference as "a program that few women can take advantage of, owing primarily to the history of sex discrimination that has restricted their opportunity in the military." The commission cited the results of Civil Service tests: women are 41 percent of those who passed the college level test, but only 27 percent of those who are hired, while veterans are only 20 percent of those who passed the test, but 34 percent of those who are hired. A Dallas woman applied for a Federal Air Traffic Controller job and scored a perfect 100 percent on the test. But she was ranked 147th in line for the job because of the automatic preference given veterans. "In this context, bias clearly breeds bias," the commission stated.

Although women are inclined to think that men have the more interesting sex role to play in life, there are men who are not so sure. They feel as trapped in their role of he-man-hunter-provider as some women feel trapped as homemakers.

"Men's traditional roles as provider and protector have dehumanized, damaged, and limited men in ways as serious and pervasive as the reproducer, sex object, and motherhood roles have done to women," says a Massachusetts man who started a crusade for "men's rights," insisting that the notion that it is a "man's world" is as false as the notion that "women are on a pedestal." It's neither a man's world nor a woman's world now as he sees it.

"To compare male exploitation of women with, for example, white exploitation of blacks is misleading. It has been a mutual exploitation, with males being taught to love and serve women in ways that whites are never taught to treat blacks."

One of the ways this man fought exploitation of males and females might at first seem petty to other people. But his logic is correct. He succeeded in eliminating a so-called advantage for women at a pub. Beers at the pub cost men 75 cents, but on ladies night they cost women only 25 cents.

"It's important to motivate women out of their comfortable but damaging passivity in establishing relationships," he said. "Ladies' night perpetuated their status as a confusing combination of honored prize and subhuman prey." And the men, relegated to the "predator role" in such an arrangement tended to become aggressive and lose their self-esteem if they did not succeed in picking up a woman.

Men's awareness of how sexism robs them of part of their humanity is growing. These are men who are secure enough not to need constant reinforcement of their worth by feeling superior to others. These are men who do not define themselves as human beings by the power or money that separates them from others.

Men of the Church

In the Catholic Church there is the epitome of male separateness. This ancient and highly visible church actually has a male caste in its priesthood, an ancient and highly visible sign of male superiority.

Segregated in adolescence or young manhood for theological training, candidates for the priesthood came to depend on the fellowship of other males, and they conformed professionally to a rigid hierarchy made up exclusively of males. Women were strangers to them. When they became priests, men lived alone or with other priests. Celibacy was a requirement for being there. Intimacy with women was not permitted; it would cause temptation or scandal.

This system may have its efficiencies and discipline, but it did little to encourage priests to understand women as equal persons. Yet women dutifully sought these men out as confessors and counselors, even to the point of relying on them as authorities on birth control.

By the time this male hierarchy was confronted with the task of answering a public call to ordain women to the priesthood, it had been inbred with maleness so deeply that the Vatican actually declared only males could represent Christ. If Jesus had intended women to be priests, then he would have ordained them or at least selected them to be among the twelve Apostles, supporting scholars argued, in an effort to raise the level of defense.

Of course, Jesus ordained no one to be a priest, and there was no priesthood as we think of it until hundreds of years after his death. Furthermore, in the early church, official orders were more inclusive of women than they are today.

Because of this over-emphasis on maleness in the priesthood, some women have argued that as priests they could bring special "feminine" qualities to the priesthood that would enhance the priesthood. This line of argument could eventually be self-defeating. Essentially it relies on the old idea of separateness, masculine virtues versus feminine virtues. As Elisabeth Schussler Fiorenza told the Baltimore Women's Ordination Conference in 1978:

> The argument that women should be ordained in order to complement the masculine ministry of the church could be fatal for women's equality in the church and make impossible a nonsexist future of the church. Those arguing for the ordination of women on the basis of women's special nature and particular feminine gifts are in danger of providing a theological justification for the exclusion of women from the sacramental priesthood and relegating women to "feminine" subsidiary ministries. While the so-called feminine qualities must be intrinsic to the

priesthood of women and men because they are Christian values, their privatization and distortion by sexism must first be confronted.

Yet even within the male-only territory of the priesthood there are men who identify sexism as injustice and call it by its name. These men are signs of hope and encouragement for women.

9

Women and Men Together

It seems so simple. Equality. A wonderful place where the perfectly equal couple live with their nonsexist children in harmony. In the morning he goes off to work—to a "fulfilling" job with upward mobility and a just salary. And so does *she.* At night they return and prepare dinner together, sipping chablis as they chop onions and salad greens, chattering over the interesting events of their day. The children have already tidied the house and completed their homework. (They are A students, and they play piano, violin, flute, guitar, and kazoo. They are also perfectly adjusted psychologically, and they never fight.) After dinner—which, by the way, is graced with witty and instructive conversation about world affairs—the children do the dishes, the husband throws a load of laundry in the washer, and the mother sits down to make a few phone calls for her church committee.

What that mother doesn't know is that in just a few minutes it will be 5:30 a.m. Her alarm clock will shatter this pleasant dream, and a busy woman's real-life world will start anew.

There is nothing simple about equality. Not in practice anyway.

For a start, that happy Equality Family probably will begin its day stumbling over one another as they get dressed, gulp orange juice, and scramble to get to work and school on time. At work the father may agonize over a job promotion that would require the family to move to another city. His wife, who likes her own job, is not eager to move. When they get home at night there may not only be dinner to make, but meetings to attend at their children's schools, bills to pay, socks to be paired, and a daughter who is angry because she is sure that she has the misfortune of having the "only mother" who will not attend the performance at her school at 2 p.m. tomorrow. By the time the Equality Family turns in for the night, it will be later than they wish, and they will be exhausted.

The road to equality is strewn with conflicts guaranteed to disrupt the comfort of our traditional routines. To make the journey together, men and women need to believe that the destination is worth the strain.

"Men are not going to accept it; it's going to have to be pushed down their throats. It scares them!" is how the idea of equal marriage was summed up by one young man from a working-class neighborhood of Brooklyn. He took over household responsibilities and care of a daughter while his wife worked outside the home. His pals thought he was strange. But he himself rather liked the time spent at home, and he learned to some degree what it felt like to walk in his wife's shoes. The experience, he and his wife both say, changed their relationship—for the better.

Not all women are willing to accept equality either. Some of them are willing to accept additional rights that equality might bring—the right to expect their husbands to share housework, for instance. Yet these same women may jealously guard their assumed prerogative to decide what foods go on the grocery list or what fabric goes on the sofa.

The basic assumption in marriage used to be that the man would provide the income, and the woman would work at home. They had separate "spheres." That is no longer a basic assumption in many marriages today. And there is a strain because of it.

Married couples now have to seriously deal with such issues as who does the dishes, who does the shopping, who changes the baby's diapers. The mere fact that a woman is working outside the home does not bring about equality. Equality itself requires work. Backsliding into traditional sex roles is inevitable from time to time, and so is failure. But men and women today can *strive* for equality. By starting to change their own lives they make the most meaningful and specific contribution they can to bring equality to reality.

One of the most difficult and elementary challenges posed by the ideal of equality is in the love relationship between man and woman. In her book, *Kiss Sleeping Beauty Good-Bye,* Madonna Kolbenschlag describes how the "sleeping beauty" experience, a common one among young women, results in a young woman's dreaming that her life will be given meaning by one special true love who will swoop her up to live happily ever after. Much earlier Betty Friedan revealed, in the *Feminine Mystique,* that where the true love actually took the young woman was to the suburbs where, instead of living happily ever after, she eventually became middle-aged and miserable.

In a relationship of equality, there is no room for a love built only on promises of living happily ever after—and, it turns out, living for love itself. There is instead, first of all, truth. Then there is justice. And then there are equal partners who are equally committed to a truthful love that grows in a just structure. In a relationship of equality, the truth includes agreement that there are no "happily-ever-afters."

There is happiness, yes. But there is also likely to be sorrow and hardships of various sorts. There will surely be sacrifices, but they will be made by both partners. "For better or for worse," yes—but always faced in truth for what it is. A mutual commitment to such a relationship is what keeps people going. And a belief that an honest relationship of equals is better than the alternatives.

The Consequences of Equality

Otherwise intelligent, logical men have in the past opposed the idea of equality because they could actually foresee the changes that would be required in the patriarchal structure of civilization if women ever came to be considered men's equals and not just their separate-but-equals.

The prevailing order in America was legally upset when the idea of separate but equal was declared inconsistent with the U.S. Constitution. Nevertheless, the practice of separate but equal continues. The changes that men foresee if separateness for women is eliminated boggles their logical minds. Giving such people the benefit of the doubt as far as sincerity goes, perhaps what they see with logic is just more than they can process through the experiences of their personal lives.

The consequences of equality *are* revolutionary. And the makings of the revolution are in the kitchen sink. Putting it in Christian terms, let's say, the kitchen sink holds the redemptive waters of equality. Just consider this typical family scene repeated in homes across the country:

The family Thanksgiving Day feast is completed. It was, everyone agrees, spectacular. Every year it is spectacular. The hostess has worked for days preparing food and cleaning the house for this occasion. *Every year* she works for days preparing food and cleaning the house for this occasion. Now, the food consumed, the elegance of the table ravished, the women of the family rise to do the dishes. Grandmother, mother, aunts, all of them rise and begin the clean-up ritual. The men stay seated. They exert themselves perhaps to smoke pipes or play cards. By what law of nature or logic is this so? And yet, it is as common at Thanksgiving as pumpkin pie.

Fortunately, in some homes, this scene is starting to change. Men are sharing the mundane tasks they used to assume were women's work. And women are learning to ask men to share the work if the men don't offer first.

But other women are confused. They are not sure they want men in *their* kitchens. Equality does require us to rethink the habits and assumptions of our lives. There are consequences of equality, and if we want equality, we have to accept those consequences.

Among the habits that make little sense under a system of equality are small things such as the expectation that men must always pick up the tab when dating women or that perfectly able-bodied women should remain seated in cars while men rush to open doors for them. "But I *like* being treated like a woman!" some of the species protest when they hear such things.

The trouble with these simple niceties is that they are tied to the notion of women being on pedestals, and that notion, as we now know, is closely tied to the idea of male superiority-female inferiority, which is a key to an authoritarian order that manifests discrimination based not only on sex but also on class and race. We should never forget to wonder how many defenders of chivalry have held doors and picked up checks for women who were black or Indian. As

Sojourner Truth once said so eloquently, "Nobody ever helps me into carriages or over puddles, or gives me the best place—and ain't I a woman?"

The price of chivalry is high. Women should contemplate the undersides of their pedestals before they permit themselves to be so elevated by chivalry.

On the other hand, there is plenty of room for straightforward courtesy and respect in a system of equality. Men and women ought to show it to one another. For instance, it is just simple courtesy to open a door for another person, and women can do it as easily as men can.

These days, when men and women are at various stages of moving toward relationships of equality, the simple door-opening courtesy has become an amusing case study in attitudes. You are never quite sure what to expect as you approach a door with a member of the opposite sex. If *he* holds the door for her, he wonders whether she will assume he is sexist. If he doesn't hold the door for her, will she assume he is rude? But if *she* holds the door for him, she wonders, will he feel his masculinity threatened? If she doesn't do it, will he think she is signaling a sort of "femininity" she doesn't intend? Or will he think she's a thoughtless feminist? It's all pretty silly. Yet it does indicate the sort of rethinking process now going on as men and women try to straighten out their expectations of one another in order to make their behavior conform to the lives of equal partners.

The same process is going on in more important ways, too. Women seeking equality with their husbands have often thought they would find it in the labor force. But merely "going back to work"—as it was called, as if homemakers do not work—sometimes has trapped women deeper in inequality.

It is a common experience for a woman to return from a full day of work at the office only to begin a full night of housework. The mere fact of her employment does not inspire her husband to assume half of the child care or housework. Moreover, the responsibility for obtaining child care is in *her* hands. If the children are sick, *she* stays home from work, not her husband. She has two jobs instead of one. She does not have equality.

If she complains, her husband may justify the situation by pointing out to her that his paycheck contribution to the family far exceeds hers. Perhaps he may say, he will consider a more equal distribution of household chores when there is a more equal contribution of incomes. A few professional women, able to earn high incomes, have found that as their incomes increased so did the equal sharing of housework with their husbands. But equality based on financial worth is a catch-22 situation. The more time and energy spent on housework, the less time and energy available for paid employment and the smaller the opportunities for advancement. Considering that women historically and currently occupy the low-paying end of the labor force, women will have a hard time achieving equality if it is based only on financial worth.

A return to the labor force has led some women to fall into another trap that prevents them from achieving equality in their marriages. The women assume that the new income they are earning is their own to spend as they wish, but they don't extend the same privilege to their husbands. They continue to assume that their husbands' incomes belong to the entire family. Such inconsistency defeats equality, and such women will never achieve partnership with their husbands unless they work out more equitable ways of sharing resources as well as work.

Still, a woman's working outside the home is frequently a step toward a more equal marriage relationship.

One woman who had always thought of herself as "liberated" found herself experiencing some strange emotions because she had wrongly assumed that her return to the labor force after the birth of her children would make everything equal in her marriage. Shortly after she obtained a job her husband lost his. Suddenly it was her husband who was home caring for little children and she who was going away every morning.

"He was making an honest effort to keep things running smoothly on the homefront at the same time he was looking for a new job," she recalled. "But as the months went by I started experiencing strange new feelings when I walked in the door at night. I wondered what he had been doing all day that the living room was such a mess or that the dishes weren't done. And I started to feel a little resentful. Here I was supporting the family, and the least he could have done was take care of the house! I was ashamed to discover that I was developing the same attitude toward my husband that I've always criticized men for having towards their wives."

The experience taught the woman that the equality she was seeking had to be based on something besides employment outside the home and economic power.

Moreover the experience with unemployment taught her husband a lesson about the contribution of homemakers to families. For the first time in their marriage, he had a chance to walk in his wife's shoes, just as she was having a chance to walk in his shoes. He found that days spent at home with small children went amazingly fast, so fast he couldn't complete the many tasks he had planned. "There are so many interruptions!" he found himself complaining. Where did time go?

For both of them this time in their lives increased their understanding of one another and moved them closer to equality in their marriage relationship.

In discussing the consequences of equality, however, we know that not all the consequences are private family matters. Equality also requires changes in public policy.

For example, there is no way we can claim equality and still justify drafting only young men for military service. Equal rights for women without equal responsibilities? That would be unfair—and unlikely ever to happen.

We cannot have it both ways, though. And the alternative to equality is to embrace again a system that is sexist at its core, a system in which women trade their human rights for protection—and discover usually too late in life, that they are not as protected as they thought.

Rethinking Christian Marriage

The equality of men and women faces its severest test in marriage. There an individual's needs and desires often conflict with another individual's needs and desires. If there are children, the well-being of the family may present even more conflicts or pressures.

While it is true that some radical feminists have been among those who have actually called for the abolition of marriage and the family, because they believe it is always harmful for women, *most* feminists along with most other people reject this reasoning. They recognize the importance of the family in nurturing children and adults, and they recognize the natural desire men and women have to commit themselves to one another for mutual support. Marriage and family, they say instead, must be reformed on the basis of equality for the benefit of men, women, and children.

When two early advocates of women's rights, Lucy Stone and Henry Blackwell, were married in 1855 they read a statement at their wedding pointing out the need for justice in the marriage relationship:

> While we acknowledge our mutual affection by publicly assuming the relationship of husband and wife . . . we deem it a duty to declare that this act on our part implies no sanction of, nor promise of voluntary obedience to, such of the present laws of marriage as refuse to recognize the wife as an independent, rational being, while they confer upon the husband an injurious and unnatural superiority. . . . We protest especially against the laws which give the husband:
>
> 1. The custody of the wife's person.
>
> 2. The exclusive control and guardianship of their children.
>
> 3. The sole ownership of her personal and use of her real estate, unless previously settled upon her, or placed in the hands of trustees, as in the case of minors, lunatics, and idiots.
>
> 4. The absolute right to the product of her industry.
>
> 5. Also against laws which give to the widower so much larger and more permanent an interest in the property of his deceased wife than they give to the widow in that of the deceased husband.
>
> 6. Finally, against the whole system by which "the legal existence of the wife is suspended during marriage" so that, in most states, she neither has a legal part in the choice of her

residence, nor can she make a will, nor sue or be sued in her own name, nor inherit property.

Men and women entering marriage today would be wise to follow the example of Henry Blackwell and Lucy Stone by making it clear in the beginning how with love and justice they intend to build a marriage and live their lives together.

But what about *Christian* marriage? Christian marriage—or Jewish marriage for that matter—is a solemn institution, not something to be reformed by whimsy or fashion.

A Christian marriage is supposed to involve three persons, not two. The third person is Jesus, and the other two persons are committed to following his teachings. And Jesus' teachings do not lead married couples through a forest of temporarily fashionable societal notions masquerading as the latest edition of truth.

However Jesus does lead men and women to follow a path of justice in all their relationships. And there are many Christians now, men and women alike, who believe that during his ministry Jesus began to call men and women to a new order between them and that he continues that same call today. It is time, then, for Christians to rethink and rework their ideas of Christian marriage.

For a start, we might rethink our prejudice that there is something wrong with people who do not marry. Singleness ought to be a respectable, valued option, not just a "leftover" or "left out" state. The intimacy of marriage is not for everyone. Nor is parenthood. Those who belong to churches ought to find ways to assure that over-emphasis on traditional family units does not exclude single adults.

We should also rethink the idea that there is something wrong with married couples who do not have children. Reproduction is not the only way that men and women can contribute to the life of a community of people. There are those individuals whose creativity flourish unimpeded by the demands of raising children. We are judgmental when we label them "selfish" for liking their lives this way. They may be wise. At any rate, peer pressure is the wrong reason for having children.

Still, most men and women will continue to seek marriage and children and hope to find happiness in this way. Many of them will look for moral support for their families in church communities, for the pressures on families will continue to be severe, financially and emotionally. Their chances for success with family life could be increased by support for the concept of equality in marriage.

Traditional ideas about the role of women or the role of men in marriage should be laid aside. In a marriage of equality there is no head, but there are equal partners. One partner should not be called to "submit" to the other. Rather they should strive to negotiate and compromise when they disagree.

All the answers for an equal marriage are not found in church dogma. And they are not all found in current feminist dogma either. People committed to the idea of an equal marriage will be often exploring new territory without the aid of reliable maps. They will have the glowing reports of the territory from the pioneers in equal marriage. And just as Columbus had naysayers who warned him that he would fall off the edge of the earth if he sailed too far west, people headed for equality in their marriage have plenty of warnings that they are on a doomed course.

There are guidebooks written to give them practical suggestions. (*Equal Marriage* by Richard Bright and Jean Stapleton is a good one.) But mostly they are on their own. For guideposts they can consult the principles of equality advanced by the women's movement. But if their ideal is a Christian marriage of equality, they will find principles of love and justice in the Bible on which to base their commitment to one another.

Whether both or one partner should work outside the home, whether the man or the woman ought to choose a career as homemaker when a family can afford it, how decisions can be made together or divided—these are matters that individual couples must work out for themselves. As they work these things out they should avoid automatically resorting to familiar old sex roles, assigning duties such as cleaning or car washing on the basis of "woman's work" or "man's work." They should think in terms of aptitude, ability, or gifts. Christians ought to remember the call to proper stewardship of their talents.

There will surely be more than one way in which people will work out the principles of equality in marriage. That is already obvious. As married couples work out new ways of being a family, it will be important for the communities to which they belong to find new ways to support them. At least it will be important if those communities truly prize the ideals of marriage and family.

Churches are communities of people that have prized these ideals most highly. And so it is important for church communities to rethink and perhaps rework the ways in which they support this ideal. Does this support extend to those families built on the equality of men and women or groping toward such equality?

Sometimes, even with the best of intentions, religious leaders send out some mixed messages about equality. On the one hand, they recognize what they call the undeniable equality of men and women. On the other hand, they talk about a principle of "complementarity"—implying that men and women have separate virtues and talents based on sex that complement one another in marriage.

There are many enthusiastic supporters of complementarity, but others are suspicious of it. "Complementarity" is reminiscent of the idea that men and women are equal but separate, and it provides continued justification for keeping the sexes confined to separate roles.

The church has come to the defense of women's right to choose the role of homemaker in marriage. And this is fine. But it turns out to be one more mixed message to women unless the church also calls for legal assurances that a woman's social and economic status are not undermined when marriage ends. Some would add that the message will continue to be a mixed message unless the church also defends the right of men to choose homemaking careers.

The best situation, of course, is for people to build a basis for equal marriage before they actually marry. Churches which offer marriage preparation classes can be helpful to people in this way. While preparing for marriage the couple should be encouraged to discuss their expectations of one another thoroughly. Honest probing could help them get off to a good start, or it might show them the impossibility of their expectations of one another, thereby preventing some potentially difficult marriages from ever taking place. Couples should also discuss their expectations of marriage. What do they hope to get out of it besides love? Do they both want to have children? If so, who will care for those children? How will they earn an income? How will they share the work?

People preparing for marriage, even those preparing for a Christian marriage in which they pledge themselves to one another "until death do us part," need to know what the reality of the institution of marriage is today. They need to know that divorce statistics are staggering, one out of three marriages ending in divorce. And they need to learn from wise people who have been divorced why some marriages have failed, just as they need to hear from wise people whose marriages not only have survived but have been satisfying. They need to know that if one partner decides to contribute to the marriage by being a full-time homemaker what the consequences of that decision may be should the other partner die or become unable to work. And they should be guided in making plans to compensate for the homemaker's economic vulnerability. Perhaps these pre-marriage discussions do not sound very romantic, but they are the sort of thing the genuine love between equal partners requires.

There are many other ways in which the church can support the ideal of equality in marriage:

- Those who give sermons for example, could start by declaring a moratorium on Mothers' Day and Fathers' Day sermons, far too many of which fall thoughtlessly into the comfortable old rut where cliches extol the selfless motherly virtues of patience and kindness or the strong fatherly virtues of hard work and wise authority.

- Married people should be involved in a real—not token—way when religious leaders are formulating teachings that affect married people, such as theologies of marriage or birth control.

- Divorced people ought to be involved, too. They have had experience with marriage, and many of them have insights that may be helpful to others in the community. Divorce, the death of marriage, is always a serious matter within the ideal of Christian marriage where it is believed that what God has joined together, people should not put asunder. Some churches do better than others when it comes to ministering to divorced members of their communities, but generally speaking there is room for a great deal of improvement in this area. Facing the reality that marriages do sometimes die and that men, women, and children commonly endure pain because of it (and not infrequently also endure injustice), is a first step for communities to show compassion and support for people involved in divorce.

● Single parents, too, need the support of church communities at least as much and often more than married couples. Communities which value the equality of persons and recognize the preference for children to have both mother and father and children's need to have both male and female role models, should have a special concern for single parents who must do alone the work of two. This includes providing single parents with friendship to ease the loneliness they inevitably feel at times. And it includes providing the children of these parents with a warm, inclusive community in which they can find a variety of adult role models of both sexes and in which they can experience the security of belonging.

There are estimates that before long one out of two children in the United States will at some time live with only one parent. This startling statistic poses a tremendous challenge for religious communities that want to be communities where parents and children are supported. Because of this, it is really distressing to see Christians arguing, as they do now, about rigid definitions of what constitutes a family. "The unmarried mother with her child or children is not a family, and never was . . ." wrote a priest-columnist for a diocesan newspaper. One is left with only sadness for the single parents, most of whom are women, who should ever make the mistake of seeking affirmation from such a man.

Equality for Their Sake

A commitment to equality between a man and a woman in marriage involves a commitment to nonsexist childrearing. Children are to be raised in a way that will encourage them to like themselves and be the best persons they can become, freely using all the talents they have. If a boy wants to be a ballet dancer, so be it. If a girl wants to become an electrician, so be it. And if a boy wants to be the proverbial fireman or a girl wants to be a nurse, so be it, also. The point is to raise them, as much as is humanly possible, to believe all options are open to them, depending on their talents and efforts. And, most importantly, to be sure that interests they have or choices they make are not discouraged "because he's a boy" or "because she's a girl."

The very best way to raise nonsexist children is to have them observe at close hand a relationship of an equal mother and father. If they discern mutual respect between their parents and see an equal sharing in decision making and work, they will have invaluable role models for their own futures. But if they only get lectures about the importance of nonsexist attitudes or if they get lessons about equality only in the classroom, and do not see equality in action at home, they will be aware of the contradiction.

When a couple attempts to raise their children in a nonsexist manner, they soon learn about the roadblocks. When children are small enough to appreciate only "Sesame Street" or "Mr. Roger's Neighborhood" on television, problems are minimal, for both shows are sensitive about avoiding sex stereotypes as well as racial stereotypes. Positive role models for boys and girls are provided. But, oh, the day those preschoolers discover cartoons! Then they find by flicking the channel old reruns of "I Love Lucy" and every other old television series that depict women as empty-headed talking dolls and men as long-suffering, all-knowing, take-charge heros. Later they will find out that in the late night shows that are on after their bedtime, all women are no older that 25, wear sexy clothes, cry a lot, and still need the help of a man to get them out of this predicament or that. Men are, of course, rugged, worldly, and usually work as policemen.

Television and sometimes a child's experiences at school can be tough competition for a parent bent on helping a child develop healthy, truthful attitudes about his or her own sex as well as about the opposite sex. It is difficult for most people to forbid a child to watch television and practically impossible to keep the child out of school, so parents have to be alert. When a child expresses sexist attitudes or behavior it is an opportunity to discuss with the child the meaning behind the attitude or behavior and why it isn't acceptable. Whenever possible, parents ought to watch television with their children and discuss with them the blatant or subtle sexism they see. (This works well for violence, too.)

It does take more effort for parents to raise nonsexist children than it does to merely repeat the pattern most of us were exposed to in our own childhood. But the effort is a gift to our children, a gift that we hope will enable them to be freer, more complete beings than they would have been otherwise.

But there are also benefits for parents who raise their children with a commitment to equality. Fathers are more involved with their children than they are under an old system that places more or even most of the child-raising responsibility on the mother, assigning the father responsibility for earning money to support the family. And, as it worked out in too many families, responsibility for very little more. Some boys have been as socialized to disassociate themselves from such "unmanly" things as changing diapers and feeding babies as girls have been socialized to believe such activities are essential to their femininity. Fathers in an equal marriage are able to discover the warm pleasure in a cuddly baby even when the baby is soiled and soaked; the self-importance of really being needed to explain the intricacies of multiplication to a third grader; the satisfaction of hearing his son say, "Thanks for mending my shirt, Dad." Contrary to much of the criticism leveled against feminists, children raised in an equal marriage do not lose their mothers; they gain their fathers in a better way.

But along with expectations for new satisfaction in parenthood, there is always the possibility of failure. Anyone who attempts to raise nonsexist children had better be equipped with a sense of humor.

I can never forget the day my own self-inflated balloon of a nonsexist utopian family burst. As chairperson of our church's parish council, I had organized a task force to recommend ways to improve the status of women in our parish. The task force had made its report, and while I was studying it, I left it on the kitchen table. My son came along and read it. One of the recommendations in the report was that girls as well as boys be allowed to be altar servers. My son was an altar boy, and he confronted me a day later with a sly smile and a question.

"Are you trying to get girl altar boys at our church?"

"What? . . . You mean to tell me you read the task force report?"

"Yeah. And I just want to know if you're trying to get girl altar boys."

"Well, yes, that's true—among a few other things."

"Well," my pride and joy then informed me, "if you do, I've already talked to all the other guys in sixth grade, and we're gonna quit."

I couldn't believe my ears. Not only was he against me, but he was the leader of the opposition—organizing against his own mother. Part of me was proud that he had learned the value of organizing for action. But most of me wanted to send him to bed without any supper.

He redeemed himself by *making* supper many times after that. But the incident reminded me what a long road the road to equality is.

Parents trying to raise children with the conviction that women and men are equal face encounters and challenges such as this on a daily basis. But for people who believe the future of men and women together is a future based on equality, the most important work for future equality is now taking place not in state legislatures but in our own homes.

10

Agenda for Equality — A Primer

It was so much easier in the old days when we thought sexism was just a problem to assign to the personnel department. Let them hire women and pay them equal wages for equal work; then we would all be done with it.

Unfortunately it turned out to be much more complicated than that. Sexism turned out to be a vast infrastructure of lies that affects virtually all our relationships with one another. Eradicating it seems like an impossible task. Equality between men and women can seem like just another fairy tale about the relationship between the sexes— perhaps more pleasing than Cinderella but not much more realistic.

The good thing about sexism, however, is that since it does permeate almost every crevice of the human race, a person who wants to fight sexism does not have to travel to another part of the world, join the Peace Corps, or, for that matter, leave the house. Sexism can be attacked everywhere. In fact, it *must* be attacked everywhere.

And the place women must begin is with themselves.

Women

Sometimes the hardest people to convince that women and men are equal are women themselves. This is understandable if we remember the new demands that equality places on women:

● They must take responsibility for their own lives. This means they cannot seek their purpose for living through a man, nor can they be satisfied to define themselves in terms of a man—Fred's wife, Jimmy's mother, Mr. Kenny's secretary, and so on.

● They must examine their behavior for passivity. If they rely on others to make decisions for them, they will have to learn new behavior.

● In expecting men to share their power with women, women must expect to share what power they have over domestic decisions with men, too.

● Barriers separating them from other women must be overcome and differences of opinion tolerated.

● If they are women of achievement, a belief in equality means that they have a special responsibility to other women to provide encouragement, serving whenever possible as role model, mentor, or spokesperson.

Men

For once there is a problem that men know for sure they are *not* going to solve by themselves. They, too, are having to learn new behavior and change old attitudes. During the transition, men should:

● Be honest with themselves about how much they personally have invested in the status quo of unequal relationships between men and women.

● Be open to the possibility of change in relationships.

● Be willing to listen to what feminists are saying—and allow the possibility that feminists could be right.

● Be aware of the many ways in which men put women down, and avoid all of them.

Families

Some of the most important work for and against the

equality of men and women is now taking place in our families. Many men and women are changing their relationships to reflect their belief in equality. Many children are being raised in homes that stress such equal relationships, and their classmates are being raised in homes that stress the importance of traditional sex roles. The groundwork is now being laid for the progress—and conflicts—of the future.

Anti-feminists accuse women and men who believe the family needs some changing of trying to destroy the family. The truth is that some changes are needed to *strengthen* the family. The authoritarian, male-dominated family model is not working well, and we need new models—for the sake of the entire human family. We need newer, stronger families, but we do not know for sure how to get them. Among the many suggestions that have been made by people who love both the ideal of equality and the ideal of family are these:

• The marriage relationship should be an equal partnership. This includes equal regard for one another and joint decision making, and it includes giving marriage a legal basis of partnership.

• The concept that anyone in a family owns anyone else should be absolutely rejected—as well as the idea that anyone in a family is entitled to abuse anyone else.

• If one member of a family takes a homemaker's role that person should never be regarded as a servant for the group. Also, that person's future should be secured along with the rest of the family—to the extent, of course, that family income permits. This is to assure that a woman or man who chooses to be a full-time homemaker for a family is not punished later in life by being reduced to an economically vulnerable position when marriage ends or family circumstances change.

● Reject materialism. The constant pressure to acquire more and better *things* is perhaps the greatest threat to families. Decent housing, decent clothing, ample food, health care, transportation, and so on—the list of basic family needs these days is long enough. But our culture encourages us to *need* even more than the basics. Items such as dishwashers and color television sets, once considered luxuries, are now basic "needs" among middle-class folks, and we feel deprived without them. This materialism is never satisfied, and when a family becomes a family of consumers, materialism can consume *them*.

The pressure for always better, more costly symbols of material success can result in excessive pressure for higher and higher incomes in a family. This in itself puts a family under severe stress. It oftens entails sacrifices—frequent moves that uproot the family, parents absent for frequent and extended periods of time for business-related travel, things which are not always harmful to a family but which have in fact taken their toll on many.

● Simplify. Along with cutting back on the family's materialistic instincts, we need to simplify our lives as much as possible. Somehow we must find ways to reduce the amount of goods we acquire (and are then forced to maintain). We must also reduce the outside claims on our time. Families take time. For instance, is it really necessary that one's backyard resemble the courtyard of a Japanese emperor? Or would the time be better spent throwing a frisbee around with one's ten-year-old?

People committed to equality face a tough challenge—

and considerable fun—when they raise children. Whole books have already been written for them, and more books are sure to appear. But when parents are out there on the great playing field of life, they can't always rely on prepared game plans. They are often forced to punt. Among the many suggestions for raising children in families committed to equality are these:

● Parents are still the children's best role models. If parents talk equality without living it, children will notice the mixed message. On the other hand, if children grow up observing free parents who have an equal partnership arrangement without being imprisoned in sex roles, those children will have enduring models for their own adult relationships. And they will have an inheritance that money cannot provide.

● Girls are a special challenge to raise. On the one hand, we want them to grow up free to follow their individual talents and interests. On the other hand, we want them to feel good about their female bodies and the potential for those bodies to give birth some day. How do we let them know that they are free to choose to be mothers or not to choose to be mothers? How do we provide them with the emotional security to see them through the vulnerable years of their youth when they will make crucial choices about men, marriage, children, work?

There is considerable guessing and punting going on just now by people who have daughters. As well as hoping and praying, to tell the truth.

We do know we want to discourage girls from being passive and nonassertive. We want them to learn how to be part of a team effort and to succeed with a group of other girls—just as boys have long done. Hence the emphasis on girls' athletics. We try to encourage them to think about their future:

"I'm going to be a mommy."

"Oh, that's very nice. . . . What else are you going to be?"

"Do I have to be something else?"

"Well. . . . well, you never know, you might want to."

"Then I'll be a mommy and a school bus driver and a singer and a doctor and a teacher."

"You're going to be very busy, aren't you?"

"Well, I'm not going to do everything at the same time."

As I mentioned, parents of girls do a lot of punting, hoping, and praying.

Our time is well spent providing girls with role models, though. A girl who has a mother who is satisfied and to some degree at least fulfilling her potential in her employment, in her role as homemaker, or in some combination of the two, at least has a clearer idea of one option available to her. We do her an additional favor to expose her to other role models as well—in person, if that is possible; through books or television, if it is not.

In general, though, if we believe in equality, we just simply ought to be treating our children with equality: no distinctions on the basis of sex as far as chores go (no "boys jobs" or "girls' jobs") and no distinctions in privileges either.

• The raising of boys requires some rethinking, too. Again there is no substitute for a good role model. If we want our boys to grow up accepting the equality of men and women—*and willing to do their share of the housework and childcare in a marriage*—then we will be off to a good start if their fathers exemplify these traits. But if they never see their father clean a bathroom or cook a meal, what have they learned from all the talk about equality at the dinner table?

We must be careful, too, not to push boys into the same old male traps that other men are trying to escape. Ideas that boys must never cry, that boys must always be stronger than girls, that a boy is not masculine if he doesn't like football—these ideas have got to go. Our boys, just as our girls, deserve a chance to be the real people inside of themselves, to be the best they can be.

What we hope and pray for is that they can accomplish this in the future without enslaving members of their opposite sex into stereotyped roles.

● Those of us raising children and practicing a faith need to be watchful of contradictions between the values children learn at home and the values they learn at church. We would hope there would never be conflicts, but there are. In a Christian community, for example, in which boys can be altar servers, but girls cannot, there is clearly a conflict of values when boys and girls are being told they are equal at home. The conflict is serious enough that some parents search out new church communities in which to raise their families.

Sexist language is noticed by children in church, too. "I don't like it," said an 11-year-old girl one Sunday. "They always sing 'brother' in the song and they never sing 'sister.'" If only her words had been heard by people who think sexist language is a peripheral and somewhat silly issue!

Society

The effects of sexism are found in all our institutions, of course, not just the family. But too often it seems that all

175

our institutions always have more pressing business than dealing with "women's issues."

"Women's issues" is fast becoming a code term. To too many people "women's issues" mean issues that aren't very important, things of interest mainly to "those crazy feminists," or issues that it "would be nice to be able to address if only—": if only the economy would improve; if only there were not a threat of war; if only it wouldn't jeopardize chances for re-election. If only.

But what some people call "women's issues" other people call elementary matters of justice. And these matters are of concern to women and men who are concerned for justice.

We will not eliminate sexism from our institutions overnight. But that is no excuse for approaching the task halfheartedly. A few of the most pressing items on a concerned citizens action agenda are these:

● *Education*—Sexism in our educational institutions is, next to the family, the principal means of passing sexism on to future generations. So it is extremely important to eliminate sexist assumptions in our educational systems— and particularly in our religious educational systems which are explicitly designed to instill values in young people.

We should not use textbooks and other educational materials that portray males and females in only sex-stereotyped roles—mother wearing an apron and cleaning house; father in a suit and tie returning from "work" to read the paper; little sister watching passively and adoringly as big brother builds a go-cart, paints a tree house, or fixes a bike.

Teachers, too, must re-examine their attitudes. And, if they are unwilling to change their opinions that include sexist assumptions, they should at least be asked to keep their opinions to themselves—just as in most schools teachers are required to keep their religious convictions out of the classrooms. (Sexist attitudes, after all, are regarded as religious convictions by a good number of fundamentalist Christians and others these days.)

It isn't fair to expect our educational systems to do alone the work of correcting the sexism for which all institutions in society are responsible. This is especially true when educational budgets are being cut and programs eliminated.

Still it is only fair to expect the principle of equality to be the guiding principle when educational budgets, programs, and priorities are set. For example, girls' athletic programs should not be regarded as frills in the educational system, while boys' athletic programs are sacred cows.

● *Business*—People who are engaged in the many different occupations known generally as "business" often refer to their environment as "the real world." And the most real thing about this real world is the "bottom line," as they call it in the real world. If the bottom line of the balance sheet isn't black—that is, showing a profit—then it doesn't make sense.

For women, business does reflect the real world, and the real world is thoroughly steeped in sexism. The overwhelming majority of women who work in the business world are at the bottom of it. Most of them are in clerical positions.

But simply requiring businesses to hire and promote more women for managerial ranks is a limited approach to equal opportunity. The requirements and the structures of businesses often work against the goals of equality. A man, for instance, may be very willing to assume half the responsibility for care of his children in order that his wife might continue in her career. Yet how many employers would permit a man to take a parental leave from his job—without his being punished by loss of seniority or opportunity for promotion? Or how many employers would understand if a father stayed home from work to care for a sick child?

Business policies and practices have tremendous impact on equality, as well as on families. In 1980, the White House Conference on Families identified liberalized employment practices as among the most important tools for keeping families together. The conference endorsed such practices as flexible work schedules and an increase in the number of part-time jobs to make it easier for workers to accommodate dual roles as parents and employees. Other practices could help, too: child-care centers near the workplace; leaves for fathers as well as mothers following childbirth; evaluation of a business' requirements for employee travel and transfers that uproot families.

Some corporations now are willing to consider—and some are willing to implement—such changes, which would help make the "real world" less sexist. But even those corporations who are not willing to change in these ways must be required to deal justly with their employees, especially their women employees. The pay that women employees receive should be equal to what male employees receive for doing comparable work. Merely by implementing that goal, the real world of business will have done something to improve the bottom line of justice.

● *Politics*—Slowly women are entering the upper levels of politics in this country after years of doing the basic political work of local organization. Yet, as one congresswoman observes, when the doors close on the smoke-filled rooms in which decisions are made, women are almost never there.

178

Of the 435 members of the House of Representatives only 19 were women; in the Senate, in 1981 only two members out of 100 were women. If women are ever to achieve the numbers and power to affect the sexism in our political structures many more women will have to run for political offices at all levels.

Yet there is a political catch-22 for women. To run for office takes extraordinary amounts of time and money these days—and most women have neither of these. Family responsibilities discourage mothers of young children from political careers even at the local level—although many of these same women have proved themselves well qualified for just such positions through their participation in neighborhood action groups and other cooperative efforts.

Women must go out of their way to support other women who do take the risks and invest in the effort to run for public office. Until women hold political power that more closely approximates the political power held by men, there will be a very hollow ring to charges of "reverse sex discrimination" when women unite with the specific goal of electing other women to leadership positions.

And with this comes a special responsibility for women who do achieve leadership—a responsibility that holds for such women no matter what their field. If these women are not dedicated to justice for women, why should we expect better of their male colleagues? Florida Senator Paula Hawkins, for example, admits of no special dedication to women's rights. She is against the ERA and recalls that feminists campaigned against her. As for the fact that there are so few women in Congress, Hawkins has observed that a person must run for office to get elected, and the fault for that lies with women not with men. Justice for women will be achieved more easily if those women who have made progress on the ladder of power offer their hands to other women below who are struggling to get sure footing.

As women do involve themselves more and more in politics they must be prepared for disagreement among themselves. And they must learn tolerance for different viewpoints along with a refusal to let their differences become additional barriers that separate them from other women.

There is a vast common ground ready for political action by equality-minded women and men. There are, for example, more than 800 sections of federal law and an uncounted number of state laws that contain examples of "substantive sex bias or sex-based terminology inconsistent with a national commitment to equal rights, responsibilities and opportunities," according to the U.S. Civil Rights Commission.

Opponents of the ERA have insisted for years that it would be preferable to change these laws state by state, or in the case of federal laws, section by section, than to pass an amendment to the Constitution aimed at eliminating sex discrimination. Now is the time for them to demonstrate their good faith by organizing state by state campaigns to bring equality to the law. A priority ought to be on strengthening the legal and economic status of the homemaker—a goal that ought to be supported by all but blatant male supremacists.

A Christian Agenda for Equality

The Christian church has played an important role in the perpetuation of sexism throughout its history. Likewise it has an important role to play in the elimination of sexism.

This includes the sexism inside the church as well as that outside the church.

But the church will not be a credible voice for eliminating external sexism until it confronts the sexism within itself.

Inside the Church: It is harder to admit injustice in ourselves than to point it out in others.

"How can you say to your brother, 'Let me take that speck out of your eye,' while all the time the plank remains in your own? You hypocrite! Remove the plank from your own eye first; then you will see clearly to take the speck from your brother's eye." (Matthew 7: 4–5) Jesus knows us well.

The church's internal justice agenda for combating sexism must be a vast one. These are some of the important actions it will need to include:

● There is a need for the church as an institution to repent of the sin of sexism before it can take steps to heal the harm done by this evil. Until there is a recognition of the sin and a repentance, it is difficult to believe that any lasting steps will be taken to correct it.

● People of the church—men, women, all levels of the church's hierarchy of people—must willingly listen to what women have to say about their experiences, just as they expect women to listen.

● Women theologians must be welcomed, encouraged, and subjected to scholarly critique as other theologians.

● Since women have been excluded from all major decision making in the church, leaders of the church should analyze the effect of past and present decisions they have made on women's lives, especially in the area of sexuality.

● Women must be given full access to all areas of service

and leadership, including, of course, ordination to the priesthood.

● Care must be taken not to emphasize women's calling as Christians to be merciful at the expense of their commitment as Christians to justice. In line with this, women must not be made to feel that seeking justice for themselves is selfish activity.

● Justice in the church necessarily includes all expressions of the church—parishes, dioceses, universities, hospitals, religious communities. All of these and others must address the sexism within their structures. This would require, for example, that hospitals and schools examine their pay scales and their promotion policies.

● Church organizations that enlist volunteer help—and most do—should beware of the tendency to regard homemakers as a ready volunteer force of cheap labor. The attitude of "we'll get some of the mothers to do that" is demeaning—first of all, to the homemaker, and secondly to the worthy concept of volunteer service. Volunteer work should continue, but only when it is designed to be a genuine service for or in the name of the faith community; when it includes opportunities for both men and women; and when it is not unjustly depriving someone else of paid employment.

● The service and treatment of nuns should be examined. Where they are regarded as professional volunteer labor and are valued principally as cheap labor, nuns should move on to new work.

● The elimination of sexist language must be given high priority in order to eliminate some of the unnecessary alienation people feel each time they participate in liturgies. In making these changes bishops and priests should not wait for mass outpouring of support from the pews. They should act boldly to eliminate alienating language in all communications of the church, liturgical or otherwise. (A practical resource book for this is *Cleaning Up Sexist Language* by the 8th Day Center for Justice, Chicago.)

● Beginning on the local levels women must be recruited for decision-making roles in church communities as well as for roles traditionally filled by men. In one of the first surveys done to determine the status of women in the parishes of a major archdiocese, women were found to be underrepresented in proportion to their numbers in all decision-making areas of the parish and in all liturgical ministries open to them. Among parish council presidents, women were only 11 percent; among ushers, only 2 percent.

Outside the Church: When the church begins to free itself from sexism, it will be an important witness against sexism in the rest of society. And its voice will be a more convincing voice when it is raised against other injustice, too. Among the many ways in which the church can combat the sexism of society are these:

● To call sexism by name. The church as individuals and as an institution contributes to truth in our society by correctly identifying, publicly naming, and refusing to rationalize sexism in any form.

On the negative side of this, representatives of the church should take care not to consciously or unconsciously contribute additional sins of sexism to the human pool—church newspapers, for example, that carry sexist jokes or, worse yet, editorials that blame the problems of the family on working mothers.

● The church should continue its advocacy for the poor, since the majority of poor people now are women and their children. This advocacy should include working for just treatment of the poor in the laws of various governments and the rules of various departments of welfare.

Justice calls the church to help defeat systems that keep people in poverty, too. And a clear vision of sexism tells us that sexism is what keeps some people in poverty. Therefore justice for the poor requires that we attack sexism.

• The church should encourage the effort to eliminate sexism in the laws. In this respect, the U.S. bishops' failure to endorse the ERA was a missed opportunity. As Bishop Michael F. McAuliffe, of Jefferson City, Missouri has said, the ERA is necessary "so that all of us can feel secure in our own hearts that women are not second-class citizens." Bishop McAuliffe, chairman of the National Conference of Catholic Bishops' Committee on Women in Society and the Church, was among the individual bishops to endorse ERA but failed to persuade the bishops to do so as a body.

"It is an interesting historical note that the bishops of the United States opposed women's suffrage when this was debated," Bishop Maurice Dingman, of DesMoines, Iowa, wrote in a letter to Catholics in his diocese. "Could we be in a similar position when the history of our time is written, and the subject is the Equal Rights Amendment?"

• Members of the church, especially those who want to affirm the role of homemaker for a family, should be on hand at legislative hearings to testify on behalf of legislation that would secure a homemaker's right to expect justice when marriage ends.

• Members of the church should be involved in healing ministries for women victims of sexism such as safe houses for battered women.

• Churches often have the resources to sponsor child care programs and after-school programs to help working parents employed outside the home and their children.

• The church has a rich treasure of Scripture and theology that it can draw upon to help its own members and others, too, find answers to the question "Who are you?" without having to resort to descriptions of the roles they perform in life. This in itself could be a great contribution to the movement for equality in our society—if the church members could avoid letting their minds and hearts be snagged on sexist passages of Scripture and theology. As Bishop McAuliffe has said:

"I believe that women must be given due consideration for the gifts and talents that they possess as humans. Too often it seems their personalities are submerged in the general roles they are supposed to play. If we could just recognize them for what they are, there would be much less suffering and anxiety in the world."

Even though the church has been a major instrument in the continuance of sexism, the church still has within it a rich healing potential for women and men.

A Challenge to Women

"I tell you," Jesus told the crowd of tax collectors, sinners, Pharisees and scribes, "there will likewise be more joy in heaven over one repentant sinner than over 99 righteous people who have no need to repent.

"What woman, if she has ten silver pieces and loses one, does not light a lamp and sweep the house in a diligent search until she has retrieved what she lost? And when she finds it, she calls in her friends and neighbors to say, 'Rejoice with me! I have found the silver piece I lost.' I tell you, there will be the same kind of joy before the angels of God over one repentant sinner.' " (Luke 15: 7–10)

This passage of Scripture tells us more than that God is merciful and that those of us who repent of our sins will be forgiven.

There is a meaning here with specific importance for women of today, we who are both victims and collaborators in sexism. Imagine for a minute that we—all of us—are the woman who has lost one of her silver pieces, something very valuable. The woman does not passively resign herself to this loss. She does not wait until her husband comes home and ask him to look for it. She does not blame it on the electrician for having wired the house poorly in the first place, thereby causing her to falter in the dim light. And she does not feel sorry for herself for being so inadequate. What does this woman do? She "diligently searches until she has retrieved what she lost"—and so should we. We women have, as a group, lost part of our selves because of a history of injustice. But we can recover it with a diligent search. There is something in those words that suggests to us that inactivity, passivity, resignation, and self-pity will not get us off the hook.

Victim, and collaborator in her own victimization, the woman in the church has a special challenge to defy the sexism that defiles her. She will do this in partnership with men, but she will not wait for men to take the lead in this venture. It will be up to woman to remove her blindfold and see that the scales of justice are not balanced. When she does that, then woman will have already begun to make the crucial first step toward a balanced relationship of equality with men.